my revision notes

AQA AS
BUSINESS

Malcolm Surridge

With thanks to all the students whose valuable feedback helped develop this book.

Hodder Education, an Hachette UK company, 338 Euston Road, London NW1 3BH

Orders

Bookpoint Ltd, 130 Milton Park, Abingdon, Oxfordshire OX14 4SB
tel: 01235 827827
fax: 01235 400401
e-mail: education@bookpoint.co.uk
Lines are open 9.00 a.m.–5.00 p.m., Monday to Saturday, with a 24-hour message answering service. You can also order through the Hodder Education website: www.hoddereducation.co.uk

© Malcolm Surridge 2012
ISBN 978-1-4441-5256-2

First printed 2012
Impression number 5 4 3 2 1
Year 2017 2016 2015 2014 2013 2012

Cover photo reproduced by permission of Yuri Arcurs/Fotolia

Typeset by Datapage, India

Printed in India

Hachette UK's policy is to use papers that are natural, renewable and recyclable products and made from wood grown in sustainable forests. The logging and manufacturing processes are expected to conform to the environmental regulations of the country of origin.

P01971

Get the most from this book

Everyone has to decide his or her own revision strategy, but it is essential to review your work, learn it and test your understanding. These Revision Notes will help you to do that in a planned way, topic by topic. Use this book as the cornerstone of your revision and don't hesitate to write in it — personalise your notes and check your progress by ticking off each section as you revise.

☑ Tick to track your progress

Use the revision planner on pages 4 and 5 to plan your revision, topic by topic. Tick each box when you have:

● revised and understood a topic
● tested yourself
● practised the exam questions and gone online to check your answers and complete the quick quizzes

You can also keep track of your revision by ticking off each topic heading in the book. You may find it helpful to add your own notes as you work through each topic.

Features to help you succeed

Examiner's tips

Throughout the book there are tips from the examiner to help you boost your final grade.

Typical mistakes

The examiner identifies the typical mistakes candidates make and explains how you can avoid them.

Now test yourself

These short, knowledge-based questions provide the first step in testing your learning. Answers are at the back of the book.

Exam practice

Practice exam questions are provided for each topic. Use them to consolidate your revision and practise your exam skills.

Definitions and key words

Clear, concise definitions of essential key terms are provided on the page where they appear.

Key words from the specification are highlighted in bold for you throughout the book.

Check your understanding

Use these questions at the end of each section to make sure that you have understood every topic. Answers are at the back of the book

Online

Go online to check and print out your answers to the exam questions and try out the extra quick quizzes at **www.therevisionbutton.co.uk/myrevisionnotes**

My revision planner

Unit 2 Managing a business

Exam practice answers and quick quizzes at **www.therevisionbutton.co.uk/myrevisionnotes**

Countdown to my exams

6–8 weeks to go

- Start by looking at the specification — make sure you know exactly what material you need to revise and the style of the examination. Use the revision planner on pages 4 and 5 to familiarise yourself with the topics.

- Organise your notes, making sure you have covered everything on the specification. The revision planner will help you to group your notes into topics.

- Work out a realistic revision plan that will allow you time for relaxation. Set aside days and times for all the subjects that you need to study, and stick to your timetable.

- Set yourself sensible targets. Break your revision down into focused sessions of around 40 minutes, divided by breaks. These Revision Notes organise the basic facts into short, memorable sections to make revising easier.

Revised ☐

4–6 weeks to go

- Read through the relevant sections of this book and refer to the examiner's tips, examiner's summaries, typical mistakes and key terms. Tick off the topics as you feel confident about them. Highlight those topics you find difficult and look at them again in detail.

- Test your understanding of each topic by working through the 'Now test yourself' and 'Check your understanding' questions in the book. Look up the answers at the back of the book.

- Make a note of any problem areas as you revise, and ask your teacher to go over these in class.

- Look at past papers. They are one of the best ways to revise and practise your exam skills. Write or prepare planned answers to the exam practice questions provided in this book. Check your answers online and try out the extra quick quizzes at **www.therevisionbutton.co.uk/ myrevisionnotes**

- Try different revision methods. For example, you can make notes using mind maps, spider diagrams or flash cards.

- Track your progress using the revision planner and give yourself a reward when you have achieved your target.

Revised ☐

One week to go

- Try to fit in at least one more timed practice of an entire past paper and seek feedback from your teacher, comparing your work closely with the mark scheme.

- Check the revision planner to make sure you haven't missed out any topics. Brush up on any areas of difficulty by talking them over with a friend or getting help from your teacher.

- Attend any revision classes put on by your teacher. Remember, he or she is an expert at preparing people for examinations.

Revised ☐

The day before the examination

- Flick through these Revision Notes for useful reminders, for example the examiner's tips, examiner's summaries, typical mistakes and key terms.

- Check the time and place of your examination.

- Make sure you have everything you need — extra pens and pencils, tissues, a watch, bottled water, sweets.

- Allow some time to relax and have an early night to ensure you are fresh and alert for the examinations.

Revised ☐

My exams

AS Business Studies Unit 1

Date: ....

Time: ....

Location: ....

AS Business Studies Unit 2

Date: ....

Time: ....

Location: ....

1 First steps in planning

Enterprise

Entrepreneurs and enterprise

Revised

An **entrepreneur** is a person who is willing to take a risk in starting a new enterprise. Entrepreneurs are important people because, by creating businesses, they provide new jobs and increase the general level of economic prosperity.

Entrepreneurs can be very different. On the one hand, those such as Richard Branson are serial entrepreneurs, creating a succession of businesses and seeing them expand. On the other, it is far more common for entrepreneurs to establish a small business and to continue to manage this business, which may only grow slowly over time, if at all.

Enterprise refers to the qualities and talents a person needs to be a successful entrepreneur. Entrepreneurs need a range of abilities if they are to succeed in establishing a business. Research has identified six key qualities of a successful entrepreneur:

- **dreamer** — having a big idea of how something can be better and different
- **innovator** — demonstrating how the idea applied outperforms current products
- **passionate** — being expressive so that the idea wins approval from others
- **risk taker** — pursuing the dream without having all the resources needed at the start
- **dogged committer** — staying with the idea through the ups and downs
- **continuous learner** — constantly exploring and evolving to do best practice

> **entrepreneur** — a person willing to take a risk in starting a new enterprise
>
> **enterprise** — the qualities and talents a person needs to be a successful entrepreneur

> **Typical mistake**
>
> Look at case studies of real-life entrepreneurs who have set up different types of business. Don't just consider the well-known entrepreneurs; look also for those who operate small businesses and non-profit businesses (or social enterprises). This will help you to judge the strengths and weaknesses of entrepreneurs in examination case studies.

Risk and rewards

Revised

Risk is the possibility of incurring some misfortune or loss. Entrepreneurs have to learn to live with risk as many new businesses fail. Surveys suggest that between 20% and 30% of new businesses do not survive their first year of trading. If a business fails, it is often the case that the entrepreneur behind it loses some or all of his or her personal wealth. New businesses can fail for a number of reasons:

- there is insufficient demand for the product
- competitors respond by taking actions to force a new enterprise out of business

- the costs of setting up and running the business may be higher than expected
- the business runs out of cash

Rewards are those things that an entrepreneur receives in return for taking the risk of starting a new business. The most obvious reward is money. Some entrepreneurs have become very rich. In 2011 Richard Branson's wealth was estimated at £2,580 million. There are other rewards too. These include being one's own boss and not answerable to anyone else, having the satisfaction of creating a business and the possibility of passing it onto your children.

Opportunity cost
Revised

Opportunity cost is the next best alternative forgone. It measures the cost of a decision in terms of what you have to give up as a consequence. Thus, the cost for you of a week's holiday in Spain might be the new clothes that you could have bought with the money instead.

Entrepreneurs take many decisions that can be measured in terms of opportunity cost. A major one is starting a business. Most entrepreneurs give up a job to start a business — the job may be well paid and have substantial benefits, such as a generous pension.

Opportunity cost can also help us to make judgements about new businesses. It is possible to evaluate the success of a new business (in financial and non-financial terms) against the income and security that the alternative job provided.

> **Opportunity cost** — the next best alternative forgone

> **Examiner's tip**
>
> Opportunity cost is an important concept. You can use it to justify an entrepreneur's decisions — i.e. they were better than the alternative.

Motives for becoming an entrepreneur
Revised

People decide to start their own businesses for many different reasons. Some of the more common ones are:

- **To become wealthy.** This is a common motivation for starting a business but only a small minority of entrepreneurs become very wealthy. However, many more earn good incomes.
- **Because they have an idea.** Some entrepreneurs have (they believe) a great and potentially lucrative idea. But it is only a great idea if it becomes a saleable product.
- **Being one's own boss.** For many people the idea of not being answerable to anyone else is attractive. This allows entrepreneurs to take their own decisions.
- **The satisfaction that results from creativity.** Establishing a new business and seeing it flourish can be highly satisfying. The idea of having a business to pass on to future generations is also very attractive.

> **Typical mistake**
>
> Do not assume all entrepreneurs start businesses to make money. Case studies are sometimes written to highlight other motives and good quality answers will recognise this.

Government support for enterprise and entrepreneurs
Revised

Entrepreneurs create jobs, sometimes in areas with high unemployment. This helps the government to meet its economic target of controlling unemployment and reduces the amount of unemployment benefit it has to pay. Entrepreneurs also pay taxes on their spending and on any profits made. Finally, new businesses place orders for goods and services with other businesses, thereby generating further revenues and taxes for the government.

UK government support for entrepreneurs takes a number of forms:

- **Education.** This entails including enterprise as a topic in the curriculum for all students at school as well as providing subsidised classes for adults.
- **Providing a business-friendly environment.** This means reducing legal barriers to starting a business and the amount of paperwork once the business is trading.
- **Financial support.** The government guarantees loans made to some small firms (reassuring banks that they will be repaid), provides venture capital to some small and medium-sized businesses and provides additional income for entrepreneurs during the crucial start-up stage of the enterprise's life.
- **Advice and information.** The government seeks to help entrepreneurs deal with the complexities of starting and managing businesses by providing guidance and training. Business Link is a good example of such support.

Now test yourself

1 List the four *most* important qualities that you think a successful entrepreneur should possess.

2 Explain briefly three reasons why a new restaurant may not survive its first year of trading.

3 Give three examples of opportunity cost that might be encountered by an entrepreneur giving up a well-paid job to become a blacksmith.

4 Outline the major reasons why people start their own businesses, apart from the desire to become wealthy.

5 Draw up a table to show the support available to entrepreneurs from (i) the government and (ii) other sources.

Answers on p. 98

Tested

Generating and protecting business ideas

The sources of business ideas — Revised

There are a number of ways in which entrepreneurs may generate business ideas:

- **Brainstorming.** A group of people make as many suggestions as possible without assessing them, which can stifle creativity. The ideas are evaluated later.
- **Inventions.** Some but not all inventions can be turned into commercial products. Trevor Baylis's wind-up radio has become a very successful product in Africa.
- **Spotting a gap in the market.** Sometimes a market niche exists that no business is supplying. A market niche is a small part of a larger market.
- **Market research.** Entrepreneurs may be conducting market research for one product and inadvertently discover that demand exists for another product.

Examiner's tip

The business described in your examination case study will be a small one with limited resources. Therefore you should only consider the ways of generating business ideas that are available to such businesses.

Purchasing a franchise — Revised

A **franchise** is the granting by one business (the **franchisor**) to another individual or business (the **franchisee**) the rights to supply its products. Purchasing a franchise normally means buying a complete business idea from someone else.

A franchise is a quick way to acquire a tested business. The franchisor can offer support and training, ongoing advice on operational issues and possibly national advertising for the chain of businesses. Buying a franchise reduces (but does not eliminate) the risk of starting a new business.

However, franchises do have distinct disadvantages. Franchisees will have to:

- keep to the business's rules on pricing, range of products, quality of product and the image of the business
- pay a large capital fee when buying the franchise and a percentage of profits thereafter

Copyrights, patents and trademarks
Revised ☐

Entrepreneurs are keen to protect business ideas from exploitation by rivals. A number of forms of protection exist:

- **Copyright.** This is the legal protection offered by the law to authors of written or recorded materials (e.g. books, films or music) for a specified period of time. Copyright gives authors and others the sole right to benefit from a work for up to 70 years and to sue any person who breaches that right.

- **Patents. Patents** give the patent holder the sole right to make and sell the product they have invented for a period of up to 20 years.

- **Trademarks.** These are the distinctive symbols, words or logos, or a combination of them, by which a business is known and recognised. They are indicated by the symbol ® and allow a business, a product or a brand to differentiate itself from competitors.

patent — grants a business the sole right to benefit from an invention for a specified period

Now test yourself
Tested ☐

6 Explain how each of the following might be used to produce a successful business idea: (i) brainstorming, (ii) inventions, (iii) market research.

7 List the advantages and disadvantages of buying a franchise as a means of starting a new business. Put your answer into the form of a table.

Answers on p. 98

From resources to goods and services

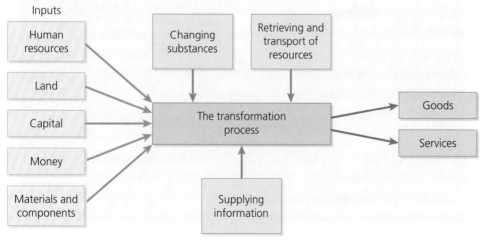

Figure 1.1 The transformation process

Inputs, outputs and the transformation process

Businesses use a range of inputs during production:

- **Human resources.** Businesses require a variety of human skills, both physical and mental. For example, a college might require the skills of lecturers, administrators, and a maintenance team to keep the buildings and grounds in good condition.

- **Land.** This is the site on which the business is based. It is important for all businesses, but particularly for agriculture, forestry or mining where land is needed to grow specific crops or to yield up certain minerals.

- **Capital.** This refers to the man-made resources used by businesses. It is a large category of inputs, encompassing machinery and vehicles, computers and furniture.

- **Money.** Cash is essential to finance day-to-day transactions and to ensure that bills can be paid on time. New businesses often find themselves short of cash.

- **Materials and components.** Manufacturers depend on supplies of raw materials and fuel, while service industries such as restaurants require food and drink to serve to customers.

The **transformation process** converts inputs into outputs. The process can take a variety of forms:

- **Changing the nature of substances.** BP and Shell convert the input of mineral oil by refining it into a form that can be used as a fuel (petrol or diesel).

- **Supplying information that is available elsewhere.** This is what a travel agent does during the process of organising a holiday.

- **Retrieving resources and transporting them.** Mining companies extract resources from the ground and transport them to places where they are used.

Examiner's tip

It is important to think about inputs, outputs and the transformation process in relation to a variety of different businesses (those in the primary, secondary and tertiary sectors of the economy). This will help to prepare you for any particular scenario that you might encounter in the examination.

Adding value

Adding value is the process of increasing the worth or value of some resources by working on them. Thus, the value of a newly manufactured garden bench is greater than the raw materials that were put into it. The process of manufacturing has added value. Firms normally seek to maximise added value, either by minimising costs or by selling for the highest possible price.

Businesses commonly add value by creating a **unique selling point** or proposition (USP) for their products. A USP allows a business to differentiate its products from others in the market. This can help the business to develop advertising campaigns and assist in encouraging brand loyalty.

adding value — the process of increasing the worth or value of some resources by working on them

unique selling point (USP) — allows a business to differentiate its products from others in the market

Developing business plans

The contents of a business plan

A **business plan** is a document detailing a business's future activities, expenditures, revenues and profits or losses. A business plan is normally produced by a business when starting or expanding its operations. The contents of a typical business plan are likely to include the following:

> **business plan** — a document detailing a business's future activities, expenditures, revenues and profits or losses

- **The type of business and the activity in which it is to be engaged.** The plan will state the legal structure of the business (e.g. a partnership) and its proposed product.

- **The market in which the product is to be sold.** The plan details the target customers, the extent of the market and the business's competitors.

- **The resources required.** The plan will identify resources such as property, machinery and raw materials as well as their forecast costs.

- **The staff required for the business.** The business plan should set out the number of employees, their roles and expected wage costs.

- **Financial forecasts.** These are a vital element of all business plans. They are based on the sales forecast (and hence on market research) and they set out the business's expected sales revenue and expenditure. The business plan should also include a cash-flow forecast.

- **Capital funding.** The plan should explain the amount of finance the business needs to purchase the resources (buildings, machinery, etc.) required. It should also state the proposed sources of funds and the entrepreneur's investment.

- **Details about the entrepreneur.** The plan should state the relevant experience and qualifications of the entrepreneur.

> **Typical mistake**
>
> Don't always write about the same elements of a business plan when answering examination questions. You should know the main contents of a plan and select the most relevant parts according to the business's circumstances.

Reasons for drawing up business plans

- **To negotiate loans.** Any potential investor in an enterprise will expect to see a detailed business plan. This helps to assess the risk in lending money and whether the business will be able to repay the loan.

- **To make a judgement.** Planning offers the entrepreneur a chance to assess the business idea in detail. At this stage, the entrepreneur may decide that it is not a good idea and abandon the plan.

- **Monitoring the business.** The plan can help to manage the business effectively. Plans set out goals or targets against which decisions can be made. So, if sales are below expectations, the entrepreneur may decide to lower the price or spend more on advertising. They also allow the entrepreneur to judge whether the business is successful. For example, has it met its sales targets?

Exam practice answers and quick quizzes at **www.therevisionbutton.co.uk/myrevisionnotes**

Sources of information and guidance Revised

Some sources of information may be expensive to use, but not as costly as making major mistakes in planning.

- **Other businesses.** Other businesses who are not direct rivals may give information on costs of machinery and other equipment needed.
- **Professionals and advisers.** Estate agents may provide information on availability of suitable property and also expected costs, while solicitors may provide information on legal requirements and expenses. Banks will supply a range of expert advice.
- **Market research.** This is often the most important source of information, especially primary market research. Potential customers can give invaluable information about whether a product meets their needs and whether it is priced correctly, and help to forecast the possible level of sales. This last piece of information is vital in constructing financial forecasts in a business plan.

Now test yourself

8 Describe the process of transforming resources into goods and services.
9 Draw a mind map to show the major types of information needed in a business plan and the sources that may be used to obtain them.
10 Compile a list of what you consider to be the five most important key terms in this chapter.

Answers on p. 98

Tested

Check your understanding   Tested

1 Define the term 'entrepreneur'.
2 For an entrepreneur, what is the difference between risk and reward?
3 Define the term 'opportunity cost' and give two business examples of this concept.
4 Why might a creative person decide to start their own business?
5 Explain two financial and two non-financial ways in which the UK government might support an entrepreneur.
6 Explain the difference between a franchise, a franchisor and a franchisee.
7 What is the difference between a copyright and a patent?
8 Why is capital needed to start a business?
9 What is meant by the term 'adding value'?
10 State three reasons why an entrepreneur might draw up a business plan for a new enterprise.

Answers on p. 98

Exam practice

Paula Morris has just resigned from a very well paid job selling dressmaking materials in a department store. She described the job as 'boring'. Paula is an experienced and talented dressmaker and has decided to start her own business. She thinks she will be a good entrepreneur but has no experience of running a business. She is trying to interest her two daughters in dressmaking and has saved £30,000.

Paula has two options for her new business. She can buy a franchise from Sew and Sew which has 30 UK outlets. None of these is near to where Paula lives, although there is an independent dressmaking shop a few miles away. This would cost £75,000 initially. Paula has not carried out any research with her customers but has decided to set up her own independent business and is receiving advice from her bank on how to draw up a business plan.

Questions

a Define the term 'entrepreneur'. [2]
b Explain two reasons why Paula might have wanted to become an entrepreneur. [6]
c Do you agree with Paula's decision to open her own clothing repair shop, rather than accept the offer of a franchise? Justify your view. [12]

Answers and quick quiz 1 online   Online

2 Looking at the market

Conducting start-up market research

Market research is the process of gathering data on potential consumers. This research can provide information on the buying habits, lifestyle and perceptions of actual and potential consumers.

> **market research** — the process of gathering data on potential consumers

Market research involves one or more of the following:

- analysis of market potential for existing products
- forecasting likely demand for new products
- sales forecasting for all products
- study of market trends
- study of market characteristics
- analysis of market shares

Market research can be separated into primary and secondary research.

Primary research   Revised ☐

Primary research collects information for the first time and for a specific purpose. Collecting primary data can be expensive and time consuming, but should be accurate and precisely what the firm requires.

> **primary research** — the collection of information for the first time and for a specific purpose

Primary market research entails asking consumers questions directly. This type of research can be carried out through:

- **Surveys.** They may be based on a face-to-face interview and a questionnaire, possibly in the high street or in a shop, or they may be conducted by telephone or post.
- **Observation.** This involves watching people in a variety of circumstances. It can provide information on how consumers might react to in-store displays, prices or the location of products.
- **Panels and group discussions.** Detailed questions are put to a small number of consumers. These are frequently used to discover consumers' attitudes to new products. They can also be used to collect information on changing consumer tastes and behaviour over time.
- **Test marketing.** This allows producers to try out a product on a small part of the market before a full-scale launch. Test marketing allows firms to iron out major faults in products before incurring the expense of a full launch.

Secondary research   Revised ☐

Secondary research collects secondary data — data that already exist and have been gathered by someone else for another purpose at another

Exam practice answers and quick quizzes at **www.therevisionbutton.co.uk/myrevisionnotes**

time. These data are relatively cheap to gather, but might be out-of-date or fail to meet the business's precise needs.

> **secondary research** — the collection of secondary data that already exist and have been used for another purpose

A wide range of potential sources of such data are available to firms:

- **Official data.** The government and other agencies, for example the Department for Business Innovation and Skills (BIS), produce vast amounts of detailed information. Key publications include the *Annual Abstract of Statistics*.
- **Trade associations and trade journals.** These supply valuable and specific information on market trends.
- **Internet.** The internet allows access to vast amounts of information about markets and consumer behaviour.

Qualitative research
Revised

Qualitative market research is designed to discover the attitudes and opinions of consumers that influence their purchasing behaviour. It reveals the reasons why consumers behave in particular ways, allowing businesses to design products that are more appealing to consumers. Qualitative research is based on the views of relatively small numbers of people and uses techniques such as consumer panels. It can be an expensive form of market research.

> **qualitative market research** — research into the attitudes and opinions of consumers that influence their purchasing behaviour

Quantitative research
Revised

Quantitative market research is the collection of information on consumer views and behaviour that can be analysed statistically. Whereas qualitative market research discovers 'why', this type of research reveals 'how many'. It provides information on estimated sales, the size of the market and the prices that consumers may be willing to pay. Quantitative research can be conducted through primary and secondary market research.

> **quantitative market research** — the collection of information on consumer views and behaviour that can be analysed statistically

Samples and sampling
Revised

A business will not collect information from all its potential consumers. This would be too expensive and time consuming. Firms need to select a sample that is representative of the whole target market (called the population). **Sampling** is the selection of a representative group of consumers from a larger population.

> **sampling** — the selection of a representative group of consumers from a larger population

The general principle is that the larger the sample is, the more accurate the results are likely to be.

There are a number of ways in which samples can be collected:

- **Random sampling** means that each member of the population has an equal chance of being included. This is appropriate when a firm is researching a product aimed at a large target group. Computers are often used to select people randomly.
- **Stratified random sampling** separates the population into segments or strata. This approach can avoid bias by ensuring that

> **Examiner's tip**
>
> It is not enough to know the various methods of market research. You need to be able to make some assessment of their value in particular circumstances.

the composition of the sample accurately reflects that of the entire population.

- **Quota sampling** splits the population into a number of groups, each sharing common characteristics. For example, a survey might be conducted on the views of women regarding a new product, and the number of interviewees in each age category could be clearly set out. This saves money by limiting the number of respondents.

Factors influencing choice of sampling methods

Revised

The most obvious factor affecting the choice of sampling method is the amount of finance available. Businesses with larger marketing budgets will spend more and conduct research using larger samples.

Market research involves a fundamental trade-off between cost and accuracy. Firms require accurate information on which to base marketing decisions, such as:

- pricing policies
- product design
- types of promotion
- target customers at whom to aim the product

The greater the amount of information collected, the more reliable it should be, but the greater the cost to the firm. Many newly established businesses have limited budgets, yet accurate market research is invaluable in aiding decision making. Firms face a further dilemma. Even extensive and costly market research cannot guarantee unbiased data. Respondents do not always tell the truth and samples do not always reflect the entire population accurately.

> **Typical mistake**
>
> Do not think that simply stopping every third person in the street will give a genuinely random sample. This will only give you a sample of people who are in the street at that time — for example, those not at work. Selecting random samples needs careful planning.

> **Examiner's tip**
>
> When assessing a business's methods of sampling consider the costs of the chosen approach against the expected financial benefits.

Now test yourself

Tested

1. Draw up a table setting out the advantages and disadvantages of primary market research.
2. Explain the difference between qualitative and quantitative market research methods. Support your answer with examples of situations in which they may be appropriate.
3. Explain why a new business might use sampling and explain the difference between random and quota samples.

Answers on p. 99

Understanding markets

Types of market in which firms trade

Revised

A **market** is a place or a means by which buyers and sellers come together to decide prices and exchange information. Some markets exist in specific locations, such as Smithfield meat market in London, while others are conducted mainly through telephone and electronic communication, such as the market for company shares.

> **market** — a place or a means by which buyers and sellers come together to decide prices and exchange information

Markets can be classified into a range of different types:

- **Local markets.** These exist for goods and services for which it is not feasible to travel far, or for which products cannot be economically transported. Hairdressers operate in local markets.

- **National markets.** These exist for products which sell throughout the UK. Some small breweries sell bottled beer to consumers throughout the country.

- **Physical markets.** These are markets that have specific locations. Many towns and villages have weekly markets whilst others cater for people from a wider area, such as Hatton Garden in London which specialises in jewellery.

- **Electronic markets.** The internet operates as a market for many small businesses, enabling them to reach a wide customer base. eBay is a prime example.

- **Industrial markets.** In these markets, businesses sell products to other businesses. Hence they are also called **business-to-business (or B2B) markets**.

The importance of demand to start-up businesses

Revised ☐

Demand is the quantity of a good or service that consumers wish to buy over a certain time period at a given price. A sufficient level of demand is essential for a new business. Without it, the business will not generate sufficient inflows of cash to pay bills as they become due, and in the longer term it will be unlikely to make a profit. A business plan should contain evidence that there will be sufficient demand for the new enterprise's products.

> **demand** — the quantity of a good or service that consumers wish to buy over a certain time period at a given price

There are a range of factors that may influence the level of demand for a business's products:

- **The actions of competitors.** If a new business's competitors react to its arrival in the market by reducing prices, advertising more or providing special offers, it will be more difficult for the new business to attract sufficient demand.

- **Consumers' incomes.** This is a particularly important factor influencing the level of demand for some products. A new business selling jewellery or hot tubs might find that its sales depend on the level of consumers' incomes.

- **Seasonal factors.** Some products sell well at certain times of the year. A new ice-cream parlour will expect higher sales in the summer, especially in a hot summer. Opening a new business at the 'wrong' time of year may result in low levels of demand.

Good decisions by entrepreneurs can help to create demand for products. Setting the right price is important. High prices may result in few consumers; if the price is too low, the business may not receive enough revenue to pay its costs. Entrepreneurs should set a price that represents good value and which takes into account prices charged by close competitors.

Typical mistake

It is important to think about the type of product that a business is planning to sell and whether demand is likely to be seasonal. Many candidates ignore this and fail to consider that this may result in low cash inflows during some periods of the year.

Demand for the business's product also depends on the amount and effectiveness of the business's advertising. Effective advertising makes customers aware of products and boosts demand.

How and why firms segment their markets

Revised

Market segmentation involves dividing a market into identifiable submarkets, each with its own customer characteristics. For example, brewers may sell certain beers to males aged 18–30.

> **market segmentation** — dividing a market into identifiable submarkets, each with its own customer characteristics

Market segments may be based on differences in:

- demographics — age, sex or social class
- psychographics — attitudes and tastes of consumers
- geography — for example, the various regions of the UK

Firms engage in market segmentation in order to:

- allow different marketing techniques/media to be employed
- increase the profit from each market segment
- assist in identifying new marketing opportunities
- dominate certain segments
- reflect differences in customer tastes

Businesses do not want to waste money trying to sell products to uninterested groups of consumers.

Types of market segmentation

The following demographic factors form the basis of many types of market segmentation:

- **Age.** Some goods are aimed at young people, some at old. For example, music and fashion tend to be targeted at young consumers.
- **Sex.** Some products are specifically aimed at females, others at males. Magazines such as *Nuts* are promoted to reach young male audiences, for example.
- **Family size.** Family size is simply the number of family members. Family size determines the size of pack purchased and the type of product required. Breakfast cereals are sold in different-sized packages for different families.
- **Psychographic or lifestyle segmentation.** This seeks to classify people according to their values, opinions, personality characteristics and interests. It concentrates on the person rather than the product, and seeks to discover the unique lifestyles of consumers and to provide suitable products.
- **Social class.** In reality, this embraces social class and income. It is a method of segmentation that is crudely based on the occupation of the 'head of household'. It ignores second or subsequent wage earners.
- **Neighbourhood classification.** ACORN (A Classification Of Residential Neighbourhoods) identifies 38 different types of residential neighbourhood according to demographic, housing and

socioeconomic characteristics. This classifies the UK into units of 150 dwellings, with the predominant type determining the classification adopted. Major users of the system include direct-mail companies, financial institutions and utility companies.

- **Education.** This is a less useful factor on which to base segmentation because it assumes that there is a strong correlation between educational attainment, income levels and expenditure patterns. Firms target luxury products at those whom they determine to be higher income earners. Newspaper readership is often used as a guide to education levels, the assumption being that people with higher incomes read newspapers such as the *Guardian*.

Market size, growth and share

Revised

Market size

Market size is the total demand for a particular product. This can be measured in two ways.

- **By volume.** The number of products sold.
- **By value.** The amount of spending on the product. This is calculated by multiplying the average price of the product by the number of units sold. For example, the number (or volume) of two-person tents sold in England in one year might be 215,000. If they sell at an average price of £90, the size of this market in value terms will be 215,000 × £90 = £19,350,000 or £19.35 million.

Market growth

Market growth takes place when the size of a market increases. This is normally measured in percentage terms. So, if the market for two-person tents in England increases to £21 million, it will have grown in size. The rate at which the market has grown can be measured using the following formula:

$$\text{market growth rate} = \frac{\text{change in market size}}{\text{original market size}} \times 100$$

$$= \frac{\text{£1.65 million}}{\text{£19.35 million}} \times 100 = 8.53\%$$

Markets do not always grow. Sales in this market may fall from £19.35 million to £18 million. This would result in a negative growth rate. It would be −£1.35 million/£19.35 million × 100 = −6.98%.

Market share

Market share is the percentage of total sales in a market achieved by one specific firm. If a particular business has annual sales of two-person tents in England worth £1.935 million and the market size is £19.35 million, its market share could be calculated as shown below.

$$\text{market share} = \frac{\text{the business's sales}}{\text{total market sales}} \times 100$$

$$= \frac{£1.935 \text{ million}}{£19.35 \text{ million}} \times 100 = 10\%$$

If the market increases in size over a year and the business's sales rise more slowly over the same time, or even fall, then the business's market share will fall. In contrast, if the business's sales increase more rapidly than the market growth rate, its market share will rise. Market share is an important measure of a firm's success in a market. Rising market share is an important target for many businesses.

Now test yourself
Tested

4 Draw up a table to show the five different types of market that may exist. Your table should include an explanation of each type of market and two examples of firms that sell in each type of market.

5 Why is demand an important factor for a new business? Make a list of the actions that an entrepreneur could take to encourage higher levels of demand for a product.

6 Draw a mind map to show seven ways in which a business might segment its market.

7 Write down the formulae used to calculate market share and market growth rate. List two factors that might cause a business's market share to rise and two that might cause it to fall.

Answers on p. 99

Locating the business

Factors influencing start-up location decisions
Revised

Most businesses seek **locations** that will help them to make profits and, for many new businesses, a good location is vital to survive the vulnerable first few months of trading. Entrepreneurs will consider the following factors when deciding on a location:

location — the place or places in which a business is based

- **The market.** A business needs to be located near to its customers to make it as easy as possible for them to use its services or to buy its products. For example, a fast-food restaurant will want to be located in a busy area.

- **Competition.** It is common for estate agents to locate close to one another because consumers wanting to purchase a house are likely to visit all local agents. An estate agent that locates elsewhere might miss out on potential customers.

- **Infrastructure.** Some businesses require good transport links to operate effectively. Thus, a business that relies on the delivery of bulky or heavy products may want to be close to high-quality rail and road links.

- **Technology.** Many entrepreneurs seek to work from home. Writers and artists are examples of occupations where this happens. A high-speed internet connection may be a crucial factor in deciding to work from home.

- **Climate and natural resources.** This is very important for some industries, such as tourism and agriculture. A seaside hotel targeting families will want to be located near to a safe and sandy beach.

- **Suppliers.** Some businesses need to be close to their suppliers. A business that smokes fish is highly likely to locate close to a fishing port.
- **Costs.** Most new businesses will seek to minimise the costs of their location so long as it meets their requirements. This helps to generate profits.
- **Qualitative factors.** Most of the above locational factors assist a business to maximise its revenue from sales or to minimise the costs it has to pay. However, some entrepreneurs consider qualitative factors. They might wish to live in a specific location to be near friends or family, or because they enjoy the countryside or climate.

How circumstances influence these factors

Revised

Retail businesses are strongly influenced by the market and by a factor known as 'footfall': that is, they need to be in a location where there are plenty of customers passing by and possibly in an area that is known for that type of business. The market is also important in determining the location of other service businesses. It is common to find hairdressers and beauty therapists in areas near to many potential customers.

Businesses in the primary sector are heavily influenced by natural factors. A fruit farm will want suitable land and an appropriate climate. Manufacturers may depend heavily on suppliers and therefore seek to locate close to them. This might be especially true if the supplies are heavy or bulky, and therefore expensive to transport. A cider maker is likely to site its business near to apple orchards. It is probably cheaper to transport the finished cider to the market than to transport large quantities of apples.

> **Examiner's tip**
>
> The above are just general influences that are intended to help you to think about the precise needs of a business when deciding on a location. Each location decision is different and needs to be judged independently.

Now test yourself

Tested

8　Compile a list of eight factors that might influence the location decision of a new business.

9　Identify the four locational factors that would be most important for (i) a newly established take-away restaurant and (ii) a farm growing soft fruits such as raspberries.

Answers on p. 100

Check your understanding

Tested

1　List three items of information that would be included in a business plan.

2　Which normally provides better-quality data — primary market research or secondary market research?

3　A wine maker has a panel of people tasting its products and providing detailed feedback to the company. What type of market research is this?

4　A firm chooses its sample so that every person has an equal chance of being selected. What type of sampling is it using?

5　List two reasons why a new business should draw up a business plan.

6　Explain the difference between market share and market size.

7　Distinguish between segmentation and sampling.

8　State two factors that might influence a website designer when choosing a new location for an office.

9　State two sources of information that an entrepreneur might use when drawing up a business plan.

10　Why might a new business seek a low-cost location?

Answers on p. 100

Exam practice

Dilip Singh is planning to start a business manufacturing luxury organic chocolate. It is a competitive market with larger manufacturers such as Green and Black's. As a part of the planning process he has conducted extensive market research, including qualitative market research. He will only have a small marketing budget but is in the early stage of negotiations with Waitrose to stock his chocolate in its 240 UK supermarkets.

Dilip has little cash to invest in the planning of his business and is negotiating a loan from the bank and trying to persuade his wealthy brother to invest in his enterprise. He is also aware that people's views on organic chocolate are changing and may have declined recently because of the recession and its aftermath.

He is concerned that there may not be sufficient demand for his products, although his bank manager is less concerned and has agreed to a loan.

Questions

a Define the term 'qualitative market research'. [2]

b Explain two reasons why Dilip might have conducted 'extensive market research' despite not having much cash available. [6]

c Do you think that Dilip is right to worry that there might not be sufficient demand for his chocolate products? Justify your decision. [12]

Answers and quick quiz 2 online

Online

3 Other aspects of planning

Choosing a legal structure for a business

The different kinds of business fall into two broad categories: corporate and non-corporate, as shown in Table 3.1.

Table 3.1 Types of business

Non-corporate businesses	Corporate businesses
Sole traders (or sole proprietors)	Private limited companies
Partnerships	Public limited companies

Corporate businesses

Revised

Corporate businesses have a legal identity that is separate from that of their owners. Their owners benefit from limited liability. **Limited liability** restricts the financial responsibility of shareholders for a company's debts to the amount they have individually invested. It means that a company can sue and be sued and can enter into contracts. Limited liability has an important implication for the owners (shareholders) of corporate businesses because, in the event of such a business failing, the shareholders' private possessions are safe. Their liability is limited to the amount they have invested.

There are two methods by which the liability of shareholders can be limited:

- **By shares.** In this case a shareholder's liability is limited to the value of the shares that he or she has purchased. There can be no further call on the shareholder's wealth.
- **By guarantee.** Each member's liability is restricted to the amount he or she has agreed to pay in the event of the business being wound up. This is more common with not-for-profit businesses.

There are two main types of corporate company:

- **Private limited companies.** These are normally much smaller than public limited companies. Share capital must not exceed £50,000 and 'Ltd' must be included after the company's name. The shares of a private limited company cannot be bought and sold without the agreement of other shareholders. The company's shares cannot be sold on the Stock Exchange. Private limited companies are normally relatively small and are often family businesses.
- **Public limited companies.** Their shares can be traded on the Stock Exchange and bought by any business or individual. Public limited companies must have the term 'plc' after their name. They must have a minimum capital of £50,000 by law; in practice, this figure is likely to be far higher. Public limited companies have to publish more details of their financial affairs than do private limited companies.

> **corporate businesses —** businesses that have a legal identity that is separate from that of their owners
>
> **limited liability —** restricts the financial responsibility of shareholders for a company's debts to the amount they have individually invested

Typical mistake

Do not propose starting a new business as a public limited company in response to an examination question. The huge costs involved mean that this is most unlikely to happen.

Those forming a company must send two main documents to the Registrar of Companies:

- **Memorandum of Association.** This sets out details of the company's name and address and its objectives in trading.
- **Articles of Association.** This details the internal arrangements of the company, including frequency of shareholders' meetings.

Once these documents have been approved, the company receives a Certificate of Incorporation and can commence trading.

Non-corporate businesses

Revised

Non-corporate businesses and their owners are not treated as separate elements — an owner's private possessions are all at risk in the event of failure. Sole traders and partners are usually said to have **unlimited liability**. However, since 2000 it has been possible to establish limited liability partnerships (LLPs) which offer partners financial protection.

The different types of non-corporate business are:

- **Sole traders (or proprietors).** These are businesses owned by a single person, although the business may have a number of employees. Such one-person owned businesses are common in retailing and services such as plumbing and hairdressing.
- **Partnerships.** These comprise between 2 and 20 people who contribute capital and expertise to a business. A partnership is usually based on a Deed of Partnership, which states how much capital each partner has contributed, the share of profits each shall receive and the rules for electing new partners. Some partners may be 'sleeping partners', contributing capital but taking no active part in the business. Partnerships are common in the professions: for example, dentists and accountants.

The advantages and disadvantages of the various legal forms of business are shown in Table 3.2.

Not-for profit businesses

Revised

Not all businesses aim to make profits. A **not-for-profit business** is any organisation that has business objectives other than making a profit. These businesses are also called social enterprises.

Social enterprises trade in a wide range of industries and operate with a number of non-profit objectives:

- **To provide services to local communities.** Some social enterprises may remove graffiti or clean up beaches to the benefit of entire communities.
- **To give people job-related skills.** The TV chef, Jamie Oliver, runs a chain of restaurants (called 'Fifteen') with the prime objective of providing training in a variety of catering skills for young people from disadvantaged backgrounds.

not-for-profit business — an organisation that has business objectives other than making a profit

Table 3.2 The advantages and disadvantages of different legal forms of business

Type of business	Advantages	Disadvantages
Sole trader	• Simple and cheap to establish with few legal formalities. • The owner receives all the profits (if there are any). • Able to respond quickly to changes in the market. • Confidentiality is maintained as financial details do not have to be published.	• The owner is likely to be short of capital for investment and expansion. • Few assets to use as collateral to support applications for loans. • Unlimited liability. • It can be difficult for sole traders to take holidays.
Partnership	• Between them partners may have a wide range of skills and knowledge. • Partners are able to raise greater amounts of capital than sole traders. • The pressure on owners is reduced as cover is available for holidays and there is support in making decisions.	• Control is shared between the partners. • Arguments are common among partners. • There is still an absolute shortage of capital — even 20 people can only raise so much. • Unlimited liability.
Private limited company	• Shareholders benefit from limited liability. • Companies have access to greater amounts of capital. • Private limited companies are only required to divulge a limited amount of financial information. • Companies have a separate legal identity.	• Private limited companies cannot sell their shares on the Stock Exchange. • Requiring permission to sell shares limits potential for flexibility and growth. • Private limited companies have to conform to a number of expensive administrative formalities.
Public limited company	• Public limited companies can gain positive publicity as a result of trading on the Stock Exchange. • Stock Exchange quotation offers access to large amounts of capital. • Stock Exchange rules are strict and this encourages investors to part with their money. • Suppliers will be more willing to offer credit to public limited companies.	• A Stock Exchange listing means emphasis is placed on short-term financial results not long-term performance. • Public limited companies are required to publish a great deal of financial information. • Trading as a public limited company can result in hefty administrative expenses.

● **Fair-trading activities.** Some businesses import products from poor societies overseas but pay above the market price for the products, and often also invest in facilities such as education and healthcare for the exporting communities.

Now test yourself

Tested ☐

1 List as many ways as possible in which corporate businesses are different from non-corporate businesses.
2 List the advantages and disadvantages of starting a new business as a private limited company.
3 List and explain three objectives that a not-for-profit business may have.

Answers on p. 100

Raising finance

The sources of finance for start-up businesses

Revised ☐

A start-up business needs capital to purchase the assets required to start trading. The types of asset will depend upon the type of business.

Retailers may purchase a shop and stock to sell, while a garden centre would buy land and greenhouses. Start-up capital may be used for marketing costs and for recruiting and training staff.

Personal sources of finance

Many small businesses are started using the entrepreneur's own money. Some entrepreneurs might have been made redundant and have received compensation. Others use savings or inheritances. Some entrepreneurs borrow from friends and family.

Loan capital

Loan capital is finance that is used by a business which has been borrowed from external sources, such as a bank. Possible types of loan capital include:

- **Bank overdraft.** This can be straightforward to arrange. An overdraft allows a business to meet its short-term debts but is repayable on demand. It is flexible, as the business only pays interest on the amount that it borrows.

- **Short-term loans.** These are loans given for specific purposes. Charges are agreed and, as interest is always charged on the whole amount borrowed even if it is not needed, it can be more expensive than an overdraft.

- **Long-term loans.** These are used to purchase assets such as buildings that have a long life. They usually have a fixed rate of interest and can take time to arrange as well as incur a fee. A mortgage is a loan that is usually secured on land or buildings for periods of 20 years or more.

Share capital

Share capital is finance invested in a company through the purchase of shares. The sale of shares generates capital for the company. In return, shareholders are granted part-ownership of the company. They normally have the right to a say in certain company decisions and may receive a share of the company's profits (in the form of dividends), assuming that any are earned. However, if the owner of a company sells too many shares to raise capital he or she may lose control of the business, as owning more than 50% of the shares gives a shareholder control.

Venture capital

Venture capital is finance advanced to businesses judged to be relatively high risk. Financial institutions (e.g. merchant banks) often provide venture capital to start-up businesses, as do a small number of wealthy individuals, known as business angels.

The investment by venture capitalists in start-up businesses normally takes the form of loan capital and share capital.

Venture capitalists not only provide finance but also offer experience, contacts and advice when necessary to new entrepreneurs.

> **loan capital** — finance used by a business that has been borrowed from external sources, such as a bank
>
> **share capital** — finance invested in a company through the purchase of shares
>
> **venture capital** — finance advanced to businesses judged to be relatively high risk, in the form of share capital and loan capital

> **Examiner's tip**
>
> Make sure that you know the advantages and disadvantages of raising capital in the form of loans and shares. This is a very common topic for examination questions.

The relative merits of various sources of finance

Revised

Each of the sources of finance we have identified has advantages and disadvantages for entrepreneurs, as shown in Table 3.3.

Table 3.3 Sources of capital: advantages and disadvantages

Source of capital	Advantages	Disadvantages
Personal sources	• Normally allows the entrepreneur to retain complete control of the business. • May be a relatively cheap source of finance and can be interest-free.	• Is unlikely to provide large sums of finance. • Friends and family may ask for repayment of loans at short notice.
Loan capital	• Loan capital can be arranged at relatively short notice. • Some forms of loans (e.g. overdrafts) are very flexible and can be tailored to the business's needs.	• Businesses are committed to interest payments at a time when they may have relatively small earnings. • An unexpected rise in interest rates can increase a start-up business's costs.
Share capital	• This can be a relatively flexible source of finance as dividends will only be paid to shareholders if a sufficiently large profit is made. • The entrepreneur has to share profits with other owners of the business.	• If an entrepreneur sells too many shares in the company, he or she may lose control of the business. • In most circumstances, private limited companies cannot sell additional shares without the approval of all shareholders.
Venture capital	• This is a good means of raising finance for risky start-up businesses. • Venture capitalists may offer advice and guidance to new entrepreneurs in managing the business.	• A venture capitalist may want a large share of any profits in return for making an investment. • The entrepreneur and the venture capitalist may disagree over the future direction of the new business.

Which type of finance is most appropriate?

Revised ☐

Certain sources of finance are most appropriate in particular situations. Personal sources are likely to be used as part of the start-up capital for many new businesses. However, they may play a more significant role if the business requires relatively small amounts of capital (e.g. a website design business) or if the entrepreneur is wealthy.

Loans may be easier to organise and available at lower rates of interest if the business has assets, such as property, that can be used as security against the loan. This is known as collateral and would be sold by the creditor (often a bank) to repay the entire loan if the new enterprise failed to make repayments. Successful entrepreneurs may find it easier to negotiate loans.

Only companies can raise share capital — it is not possible for sole traders or partnerships to sell shares.

Venture capital is most appropriate for high-risk enterprises. A high-risk enterprise is one that has a higher than normal chance of failing. These might be enterprises that are unique, or which involve entrepreneurs with little or no experience of running a business.

Now test yourself

Tested ☐

4 Make a list of the sources of finance that are available to (i) private limited companies and (ii) sole traders and partnerships.

5 Compile a list of the circumstances in which these sources of finance may be most suitable: (i) share capital, (ii) loan capital and (iii) venture capital.

Answers on p. 100

Employing people

The types of employee used in small businesses

An entrepreneur may work alone when first starting a business. However, it is common for even the newest business to hire employees. Employees can be divided into several categories:

- **Full-time employees.** Full-time employees work in the business for a whole working week every week. The number of hours that is considered to be full time is usually between 35 and 40.
- **Part-time employees.** Part-time employees work for fewer than full-time hours each week. This may be 2 or 3 days each week or it could be shorter hours each day because of childcare responsibilities.
- **Permanent employees.** Permanent employees remain with a business until they decide to leave or their employment is ended for one of a limited number of reasons allowed by the law.
- **Temporary employees.** This category of employee is only employed for a set period of time. This is agreed at the time the employment commences. Temporary employment is commonly arranged to cover a period in which the business is particularly busy or to cover for other permanent employees who are absent from work for reasons such as maternity leave.

> **full-time employees** — employees who work in the business for a whole working week every week
>
> **part-time employees** — employees who work for fewer than full-time hours each week

> **Typical mistake**
>
> It is not unusual for students to confuse part-time and temporary employees. Make sure you have a clear understanding of the distinction.

Using consultants and advisers

Consultants and advisers have specialist skills that can be of great value to entrepreneurs, especially during the start-up stage of the business. They can offer a range of support to businesses, including:

- constructing and conducting a programme of market research
- recruiting the best available employees
- overcoming operational issues, such as providing high-quality service
- preparing business plans in support of loan applications

Consultants and advisers are normally hired to complete a specific task or tasks. They usually bring great experience to the solution of a range of business issues and problems. Hiring consultants and advisers can be expensive, but their support can be of enormous value to entrepreneurs and may help to ensure the survival of a fledgling enterprise. They may be paid a daily rate while working for the start-up business or a flat fee for completing the task.

> **Examiner's tip**
>
> One benefit of using consultants and advisers can come before the business starts trading, when they can help to decide whether a proposed enterprise is viable.

Reasons for and drawbacks of employing people

Reasons for

Employing people in their business offers significant benefits to entrepreneurs. It is unlikely that an entrepreneur will have the full range of skills necessary to manage a business successfully. Some entrepreneurs have excellent selling and marketing skills, but know little about managing finance; others might have great abilities in the areas of production and design, but limited understanding of managing and leading people. Entrepreneurs can employ people to support them and to provide the skills and knowledge they do not possess.

The workload of an entrepreneur can be immense. Working very long hours may mean an entrepreneur cannot give an optimal performance. Employing people to carry out routine duties in the business can allow for time off and also for precious holidays.

Drawbacks

Entrepreneurs have to conform with UK and European Union (EU) employment law if they employ people. This law is comprehensive and covers issues such as advertising vacancies, recruiting staff, paying employees and providing safe and healthy working environments. Employees may not carry out their duties to the standard expected, or they may fall ill, requiring prolonged periods off work. Employees may become parents and therefore be entitled to periods off work during which they have to be paid.

Employing people can bring great benefits to start-up businesses, but only if the right employees are hired.

> **Now test yourself**
>
> 6   Draw up a table to show the advantages and disadvantages of employing people under the headings of 'financial reasons' and 'non-financial reasons'.
>
> **Answers on p. 100**
>
> Tested ☐

Tested ☐

Check your understanding

1   Define the term 'corporate business'.
2   Give two examples of types of corporate businesses and two examples of types of non-corporate businesses.
3   Explain the difference between a temporary and a part-time employee.
4   State four sources of finance available to an entrepreneur starting a business as a private limited company.
5   What is the difference between an overdraft and a bank loan?
6   Why should the owner of a private limited company not sell too many shares in the business?
7   Explain one major disadvantage of forming a partnership to run a new business.
8   Why are most new businesses set up as sole traders?
9   Explain the advantage of using share capital to finance a new business.
10   Why do many new businesses rely on personal sources of finance?

Answers on p. 100

Exam practice

After much deliberation Ian and Sarah Morris eventually decided that their new restaurant would be operated as a private limited company rather than a partnership. Their decision had been based on financial benefits. It also gave them the opportunity to raise finance in the form of venture capital.

They were delighted with the property they had purchased for the restaurant as it also provided a home for themselves and their children. Sarah and Ian had sold their house to finance their enterprise and Sarah's (retired) father had invested in the business.

The restaurant is in Scarborough and they expect 60% of sales to be between May and August. Sarah is very keen to employ temporary staff in the restaurant (although they have never employed anyone before) though Ian is less keen.

Questions

a   Define the term 'venture capital'. [2]

b   Explain two benefits that Ian and Sarah might receive from employing temporary employees. [6]

c   Ian and Sarah decided to establish their business as a private limited company. Do you agree with their decision? Justify your view. [12]

Answers and quick quiz 3 online

Online

Exam practice answers and quick quizzes at **www.therevisionbutton.co.uk/myrevisionnotes**

4 Financial planning

Calculating costs, revenues and profits

Fixed, variable and total costs and their calculation

Revised

Fixed costs

Fixed costs are expenses that do not vary with changes in demand or output. They remain constant over time and have to be paid whether any products are made and sold or not. Examples of fixed costs are:

- rent
- salaries
- interest charges

Variable costs

Variable costs are those costs incurred by a business that vary directly with the level of output. Thus as output rises or falls, so do variable costs. Examples of variable costs include:

- materials and components
- power
- shop-floor labour costs

Many entrepreneurs calculate the variable cost of producing a single unit of output (for example, a bottle of wine or a single hotel guest). This figure (which is termed variable cost per unit) can then be multiplied by the number of units of output to give total variable costs. Variable cost per unit is also useful in calculating breakeven point.

Total costs

Total costs can be calculated by the formula:

total costs = fixed costs + variable costs

Entrepreneurs should know the total costs of the business, as this can help with pricing decisions. If an entrepreneur can set his or her prices at a level that covers the business's total costs, then the business will make a profit. However, this assumes that the products will sell at the chosen price and that sufficient numbers will be sold.

Figure 4.1 shows how fixed, variable and total costs alter as output increases, as well as the relationship between the three types of cost.

As total costs are the sum of fixed and variable costs, the lines representing variable and total costs are parallel in Figure 4.1. This is because the difference between them is fixed costs, which do not change when output changes.

> **fixed costs** — expenses that do not vary with changes in demand or output
>
> **variable costs** — those costs incurred by a business that vary directly with the level of output

> **Typical mistake**
>
> Students often offer incomplete definitions of variable costs in examinations. It is not enough to say that they vary with output; you must say that they vary **directly** with the level of output.

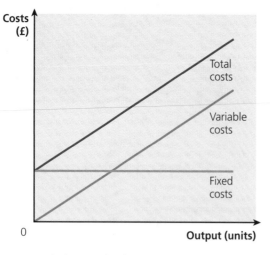

Figure 4.1 A graph showing fixed costs, variable costs and total costs

The relationship between price and total revenue

Revenue is the total value of sales made by a business over a specified period of time. This is also called sales revenue or total revenue. Revenue is calculated by using the formula:

> **revenue = quantity sold × selling price per unit**

However, there is a complex relationship between price and revenue. An increase in price does not automatically increase a business's revenue. Whether revenue increases or not following a price rise depends on how many customers stop buying the product. If a price rise leads to many customers deciding to stop buying the product, it may result in a fall in revenue. On the other hand, if most customers continue to buy the product, sales revenue will increase following a price rise.

A start-up business will benefit from market research into how sensitive the demand of potential customers is in response to changes in the price of the product.

Profit is the amount that is left over from revenue after all costs incurred in earning that revenue have been deducted. It is given by:

> **profit = sales revenue – total cost**

Calculating profit may require you to use the following formula:

> **profit = revenue – (fixed costs + variable costs)**

Some examples of how to calculate profit are shown below.

> **revenue** — the total value of sales made by a business over a specified period of time
>
> **profit** — the amount that is left over from revenue after all costs incurred in earning that revenue have been deducted

Example 1

Imagine a firm has a selling price of £10 per unit, variable cost per unit of £5 and fixed costs of £60,000.

(1) Profit or loss at output and sales of 5,000 units:

		£
Sales revenue (£10 × 5,000 units)		50,000
Variable costs (£5 × 5,000 units)	25,000	
Fixed costs	60,000	
Total costs		85,000
Loss		(35,000)

(2) Profit or loss at output and sales of 15,000 units:

		£
Sales revenue (£10 × 15,000 units)		150,000
Variable costs (£5 × 15,000 units)	75,000	
Fixed costs	60,000	
Total costs		135,000
Profit		15,000

Note how revenue and variable costs change when the level of output and sales is altered.

Knowing how to calculate the various component parts of a firm's costs, revenues and profit is, of course, important. However, it is the relationship between these parts that really allows analysis, planning and decision making to take place.

Profit is important for most entrepreneurs when starting a business. It is the reward for taking a risk in starting the business and also for those people who may have invested in it. It may be that a new business does not make a profit during the early stages of trading. It can take time to build up a sufficient customer base to generate enough revenue to cover the total costs of production.

> **Examiner's tip**
>
> Remember that some businesses do not aim to make a profit. Do not always assume this is the case when answering examination questions — it can give you an alternative line of argument.

Now test yourself

Tested

1. An entrepreneur has calculated that the fixed costs of his business are £100,000 and that variable costs per unit are £20. He has decided to increase his monthly output from 1,000 units to 2,000 units. Calculate the increase in his total costs that will result from this decision.
2. Assume that the company in Question 1 actually produces and sells 10,000 units. Calculate its profit or loss at this level of production.

Answers on p. 101

Using breakeven analysis to make decisions

Contribution and contribution per unit

Revised

Contribution

Contribution is the difference between sales revenue and variable costs. It is calculated using the following formula:

> **contribution** — the difference between sales revenue and variable costs

contribution = sales revenue − variable costs

Contribution is important to all businesses, particularly to those that produce a variety of products. It is used in the first place to pay a company's fixed costs. Once these have been covered, any additional contributions provide profits for the company.

A start-up business may plan to produce two products: A and B.

	Product A	**Product B**
Price per unit	£10	£25
Variable cost per unit	£6	£15
Forecast sales (units)	10,000	35,000
Total contribution	£40,000	£350,000

In each case, we have simply deducted the variable cost of per unit production from the selling price per unit of the product before multiplying by sales to arrive at total contribution.

Contribution per unit

The idea of contribution is that each individual product has to make a contribution to the overall running costs of the firm. As long as the selling price of an individual product is greater than the variable costs associated with making the product, the product will make a contribution to paying the overheads of the business and may eventually generate profit.

Contribution per unit can be calculated in two ways:

(1)   unit selling price – unit variable costs = contribution per unit

(2) $\dfrac{\text{total sales revenue – total variable costs}}{\text{output}}$ = contribution per unit

The meaning of breakeven and how to calculate it

Revised

Breakeven occurs at the level of output at which a business's total costs exactly equal its revenue or earnings, and neither a profit nor a loss is incurred.

At breakeven point, the business has made insufficient sales to make a profit, but sufficient sales to avoid a loss. In other words, it has earned just enough to cover its costs. This occurs when total cost = total sales revenue.

Breakeven analysis can provide businesses with important information. The most important element of this information is an indication of how much the firm needs to produce (and sell) in order to make a profit.

The breakeven point can be calculated using the formula:

breakeven in units of output = $\dfrac{\text{fixed costs}}{\text{selling price – variable cost per unit}}$

> **breakeven** — the level of output at which a business's total costs exactly equal its revenue or earnings, and neither a profit nor a loss is incurred

---

Example 3

Look again at Example 1 on page 33. The firm in question sold its products for £10 each, incurred a variable cost on each unit of £5 and had fixed costs of £60,000. Using the formula above:

$$\text{breakeven} = \frac{60,000}{(£10 - £5)} = \frac{60,000}{5} = \textbf{12,000 units}$$

Thus, if the firm produces and sells 12,000 units, its costs will exactly equal its revenues and it will break even.

Contribution and breakeven

The theory of contribution shows that if each product makes a contribution, and all these contributions are added up and used to pay fixed costs, any contribution remaining at this point is profit.

We can use the theory of contribution to calculate breakeven and profit for any given situation. The question is: how many individual contributions are needed to pay fixed costs? This is given by:

$$\frac{\textbf{fixed costs}}{\textbf{contribution per unit}} = \begin{array}{c}\textbf{number of}\\\textbf{contributions needed}\end{array} = \begin{array}{c}\textbf{level of output}\\\textbf{to break even}\end{array}$$

At this point, enough contributions have been made to pay fixed costs. Variable costs have already been accounted for because contribution = sales revenue − variable cost.

This is a very useful formula, as it enables businesses to model 'what if' scenarios quickly and easily without having to redraw breakeven charts all the time.

How to construct a breakeven chart
Revised

One way of representing the breakeven point is through the use of a breakeven chart, as shown in Figure 4.2. The step-by-step points below show how to draw a breakeven chart:

1 Give the chart a title.
2 Label axes (horizontal — output in units; vertical — costs/revenues in pounds).
3 Draw on the fixed cost line.
4 Draw on the variable cost line.
5 Draw on the total cost line.
6 Draw on the sales revenue line.
7 Label the breakeven point where sales revenue = total cost.
8 Mark on the selected operating point (SOP): that is, the actual or forecast level of the company's output.

9   Mark on the margin of safety (the difference between the SOP and the breakeven level of output).

10 Mark clearly the amount of profit and loss. Note that this is a vertical distance at any given level of production, and not an area.

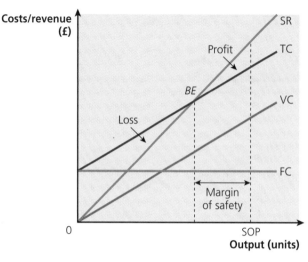

Figure 4.2 A breakeven chart for product X

Analysing the effects of changes on breakeven charts

Revised

Breakeven analysis can illustrate the effects of changes in price and costs, and assist entrepreneurs in making decisions by the use of 'what if?' scenarios:

● What level of output and sales will be needed to break even if we sell at a price of £x per unit?

● What would be the effect on the level of output and sales needed to break even of an x% rise (or fall) in fixed or variable costs?

Using breakeven analysis in this way, entrepreneurs can decide whether it is likely to be profitable to supply a product at a certain price or to start production. This aspect of breakeven analysis makes it a valuable technique. Few businesses trade in environments in which changes in prices and costs do not occur regularly.

Figure 4.3 illustrates the effects of changes in key variables on the breakeven chart. These are further illustrated in Table 4.1.

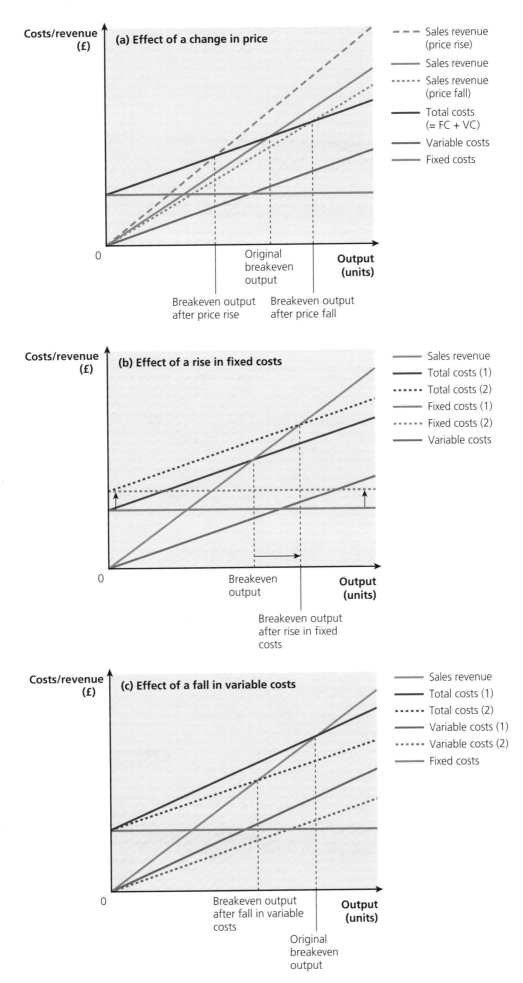

Figure 4.3 Effects of changes in key variables on the breakeven chart

Note: Figure 4.3(b) only illustrates a rise in fixed costs to avoid the diagram becoming too complex. A fall in fixed costs would have the exact opposite effect. For the same reason, Figure 4.3(c) only illustrates a fall in variable costs. A rise in variable costs would have the exact opposite effect.

Table 4.1 Effects of changes in key variables on the breakeven chart

Change in key variable	Impact on breakeven chart	Effect on breakeven output	Explanation of change	Illustrated in figure
Increase in selling price	Revenue line pivots upwards	Breakeven is reached at a lower level of output	Fewer sales will be necessary to break even because each sale generates more revenue, while costs have not altered	Figure 4.3(a)
Fall in selling price	Revenue line pivots downwards	A higher level of output is necessary to reach breakeven	Each sale will earn less revenue for the business and, because costs have not altered, more sales will be required to break even	Figure 4.3(a)
Rise in fixed costs	Parallel upward shift in fixed and total cost lines	Breakeven occurs at a higher level of output	More sales will be required to break even because the business has to pay higher costs before even starting production	Figure 4.3(b)
Fall in fixed costs	Parallel downward shift in fixed and total cost lines	Smaller output required to break even	Because the business faces lower costs, fewer sales will be needed to ensure that revenue matches costs	
Rise in variable costs	Total cost line pivots upwards	Higher output needed to break even	Each unit of output costs more to produce, so a greater number of sales will be necessary if the firm is to break even	
Fall in variable costs	Total cost line pivots downwards	Lower level of output needed to break even	Every unit of production is produced more cheaply, so less output and fewer sales are necessary to break even	Figure 4.3(c)

The strengths and weaknesses of breakeven analysis
Revised

Strengths of breakeven analysis

Breakeven analysis has the following strengths:

- **Starting a new business.** An entrepreneur can estimate the level of sales required before the business would start to make a profit. From this, the entrepreneur can see whether or not the business proposal is viable. The results of market research are important here.
- **Supporting loan applications.** Entrepreneurs will be unlikely to succeed in negotiating a loan with a bank unless they have carried out a range of financial planning, including breakeven analysis.
- **Measuring profit and losses.** In diagrammatic form, breakeven analysis enables businesses to tell at a glance what their estimated level of profit or loss would be at any level of output and sales.
- **Modelling 'what if?' scenarios.** Breakeven analysis enables businesses to model what will happen to their level of profit if they change prices or are faced by changes in costs.

Limitations of breakeven analysis

Breakeven analysis is quick to perform but it is a simplification. As such, it has several shortcomings:

- No costs are truly fixed. A stepped fixed cost line would be a better representation, as fixed costs are likely to increase in the long term and at higher levels of output if more production capacity is required.

Examiner's tip

It is common for examination questions to ask you to read data from breakeven charts. You may be required to read off profit or loss, revenue or variable costs. You should practise doing this.

- The total cost line should not be represented by a straight line because this takes no account of the discounts available for bulk buying.
- Sales revenue assumes that all output produced is sold and at a uniform price, which is unrealistic.
- The analysis is only as good as the information provided. Collecting accurate information is expensive, and in many cases the cost of collection would outweigh any benefit that breakeven analysis could provide.

Now test yourself

3 Use the information in Example 2 on p. 34 to calculate the contribution per unit for Product A and Product B.

4 Prepare a list of the following formulae used in financial planning: total costs, revenue, profit, contribution, contribution per unit and breakeven output.

5 Draw two breakeven charts to illustrate (i) a rise in fixed costs and (ii) a fall in variable costs. Label these charts accurately to show the effect on breakeven output.

Answers on p. 101

Using cash-flow forecasting

The nature of cash flow

Cash flow is the amount of money moving into and out of a business over a period of time. Cash flow is important for businesses, especially newly established businesses, because it indicates their ability to pay bills as they become due. Most new businesses will encounter periods when outflows of funds are larger than inflows. It is vital that entrepreneurs are aware of such periods and make plans to manage them.

> **cash flow** — the amount of money moving into and out of a business over a period of time

How to forecast cash flow

Cash-flow forecasts are constructed using a number of potential sources. The starting point is to use market research to establish the expected demand for the new good or service. This is more likely to be accurate if primary research is conducted. Secondary market research may also provide useful information on future inflows of cash, and may be especially helpful concerning issues such as seasonal fluctuations in sales.

Outflows of cash can be more easily estimated once the entrepreneur knows the expected levels of sales. The entrepreneur then has some idea of the amount of fuel, labour, materials and other resources that will be required.

It can often be difficult to forecast cash flows accurately for new businesses. It may not be feasible to conduct sufficient primary research because of cost or time constraints. The reactions of competitors to the arrival of the new business in the market are difficult to assess accurately. They might respond by cutting prices or launching promotional campaigns, and therefore inflows of cash for the new business may be lower than expected.

> **Examiner's tip**
>
> Avoid saying that the difference between cash inflows and outflows is profit. Cash flow relates to timing — a profitable business may run short of cash if customers do not pay on time. Many new businesses also have to spend large sums of money on advertising, materials and paying wages (creating cash outflows) some time before they receive any cash inflows. It may be that the business is very profitable once it receives payment — if it survives that long.

The structure of a cash-flow forecast

Cash-flow forecasts are a central part of a business plan for a new business. They comprise three sections:

- **Receipts** — recording the expected total month-by-month receipts.
- **Payments** — recording the expected monthly expenditure by item.
- **Running balance** — keeping a running total of the expected bank balance at the beginning and end of each month (see Figure 4.4). These are termed **opening and closing balances**. The closing balance at the end of one month becomes the opening balance at the start of the next month.

Negative figures in cash-flow forecasts are usually shown in brackets.

Month	Jan	Feb	Mar	Apr	May	June
Receipts						
1 Sales cash	4,500					
2 Sales credit	3,650					
3 Total cash in (1 + 2)	8,150					
Payments						
4 Supplies	2,500					
5 Wages	1,900					
6 Fuel	900					
7 Electricity	200					
8 Heating	200					
9 Rates	400					
10 Mortgage payment	900					
11 Interest on loan	450					
12 Total cash out (4 + 5 + 6... + 11)	7,450					
13 Net cash flow (3 − 12)	700					
14 Opening bank balance	(250)	450				
15 Closing bank balance (14 + 13)	450					

Figure 4.4 An example of a cash-flow forecast completed for the month of January

> **Typical mistake**
>
> It is not unusual for a cash-flow calculation in an examination to include negative figures. Many students have difficulty carrying out calculations involving negative figures and make errors when adding and subtracting where one or more figure is negative.

Why businesses forecast cash flow

Cash-flow forecasting is used to:

- forecast periods of time when cash outflows might exceed cash inflows, to allow entrepreneurs to take action (e.g. arranging a loan) to avoid the business being unable to pay bills on time
- plan when and how to finance major items of expenditure (e.g. vehicles or machinery), which may lead to large outflows of cash
- highlight any periods when cash surpluses may exist that could be used elsewhere
- help entrepreneurs to assess whether their business idea will generate enough cash to be able to survive
- provide evidence for lenders (e.g. banks) that any loans given can and will be repaid

Setting budgets

Structure of income, expenditure and profit budgets Revised

A **budget** is a financial plan. Its purpose is to provide a target for entrepreneurs and managers as well as a basis for a later assessment of the performance of a business. A budget should have a specific purpose and must have a set of targets attached to it if it is to be of value.

Income budgets

Income budgets are forecasted earnings from sales and are sometimes called sales budgets. For a newly established business they will be based on the results of market research. Established businesses can also call upon past trading records to provide information for sales forecasts. Income budgets are normally drawn up for the next financial year, on a monthly basis, as shown in Table 4.2.

Expenditure budgets

An **expenditure budget** sets out the expected spending of a business, broken down into a number of categories. The titles given to these categories will depend upon the type of business. A manufacturing business will have sections entitled 'Raw materials' or 'Components', whereas a service business may not. Therefore the categories in Table 4.2 may vary according to the type of business.

Profit (or loss) budgets

This budget is calculated by subtracting forecast expenditure (or costs) from forecast sales income. Depending on the balance between expenditure and income, a loss or a profit may be forecast. It is not unusual for a new business to forecast (and actually make) a loss during its first period of trading.

Table 4.2 shows forecast income, expenditure and profit/loss for a newly established manufacturer of surfboards. This extract shows forecasts for the first three months of trading.

> **budget** — a financial plan
>
> **income budget** — forecasted earnings from sales, sometimes called sales budget
>
> **expenditure budget** — the expected spending of a business

Table 4.2 Viking Boards Ltd's budget (April to June)

	April (£)	May (£)	June (£)
Cash sales	10,215	15,960	17,500
Credit sales	0	0	4,125
Total sales	**10,215**	**15,960**	**21,625**
Purchases of raw materials and components	19,500	14,010	15,550
Interest payments	1,215	1,105	1,350
Wages and salaries	3,000	2,850	2,995
Marketing and administration	2,450	2,400	2,450
Other costs	975	1,100	1,075
Total costs	**27,140**	**21,465**	**23,420**
Profit/(loss)	**(16,925)**	**(5,505)**	**(1,795)**

> **Examiner's tip**
>
> In an examination, you should be able to complete budgets such as the one shown here by inserting any missing figures, or be able to recalculate it if, for example, there is a change in the forecast income from sales.

The process of setting budgets

Revised

As Table 4.2 shows, budgets have a common structure. The top of the budget shows income, and this is followed by expenditure and finally by profit or loss. This is also the sequence in which budgets are set. Figure 4.5 summarises this process.

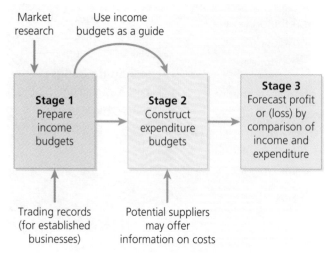

Figure 4.5 The process of setting budgets

Entrepreneurs set budgets because:

- They are an essential element of a business plan. A bank is unlikely to grant a loan without evidence of this particular form of financial planning.

- Budgets can help entrepreneurs to decide whether or not to go ahead with a business idea. If the budget shows a significant loss in its first year of trading, with little improvement evident, then the business idea may be abandoned.

- Budgets can help with pricing decisions. If a large loss is forecast, the entrepreneur may decide to sell the product at a higher price to improve the business's financial prospects.

Difficulties of setting budgets

Revised

The owner of a new business can expect to face several difficulties when drawing up a first set of budgets:

- There is no historical evidence available to an entrepreneur in setting budgets for a business start-up. It has no trading records to show the level of sales income or costs, or how these figures fluctuated throughout the year.

- Forecasting costs can also be problematic. The entrepreneur may lack the experience to estimate costs such as those for raw materials or wages.

- Competitors may respond to the appearance of a new business by cutting prices or promoting their products heavily. This can affect the sales income of the new business, as it may receive less than it forecast. The new business may have to increase expenditure on promotion, so increasing its costs.

Examiner's tip

Remember all financial information given in a Unit 1 examination paper is forecast. It may not be accurate. You should treat this with caution, especially if you think that the quality of market research was poor.

Now test yourself

6 Write brief notes to explain why it is important for the owner of a start-up business to draw up budgets, and explain why this is more difficult than for an established business.

Answers on p. 101

Tested

Assessing business start-ups

A **business objective** is a medium- to long-term target or goal of an enterprise. Objectives are normally expressed in a quantified form. People start their own businesses to achieve varied objectives:

- **To develop an idea.** An entrepreneur may also be an inventor and have developed an idea for a good or service which they want to sell commercially.

- **To run a business.** Some people want to be their own boss and to have greater control over their lives and not be answerable to other people. This is a powerful motivator for some would-be entrepreneurs.

- **To make money.** Surprisingly, research suggests that this not the most common objective among start-up entrepreneurs. Obviously some entrepreneurs do establish businesses with this objective, but it is likely to prove to be a very long-term objective. Most entrepreneurs do not become very wealthy, and of those who do, most achieve this only after years of hard work.

- **To help society.** Some enterprises (called social enterprises) are established to help the entrepreneur's community. Social enterprises may offer training and work to the unemployed, provide services to those who are disadvantaged, such as the disabled, or protect the environment.

> **business objective** — a medium- to long-term target or goal of an enterprise

Potential investors and suppliers as well as the entrepreneurs themselves are likely to have to assess the strengths and weaknesses of a business plan. What they look for may depend on the reason for their interest, but a number of common questions may be asked:

- **Will people buy the business's product?** If consumers do not want to buy the business's product, the enterprise will fail, irrespective of any other factors. Some entrepreneurs develop clever ideas, but these cannot be transformed into commercial products. A shrewd assessor will look for evidence of good-quality primary market research to provide evidence on the expected sales. He or she will also look for some assessment of the competition and how the business intends to compete with these rivals.

- **Will the business make a profit?** It is perhaps unrealistic to expect a new enterprise to make an immediate profit. Many new businesses start by incurring losses. However, investors will look for evidence that the business will make a profit over the course of several years and so offer the prospect of a good return. Evidence may be found in the form of sales forecasts and estimates of future profits.

- **Will the business run out of cash?** Cash flow poses a major problem for many start-up businesses. It may be that suppliers want to be paid on delivery, as they have no experience of trading with this business, while the entrepreneur may have to offer customers trade credit to attract them. Anyone analysing a business plan will look closely at a cash-flow forecast to judge its likely accuracy and also at plans in hand to deal with any problems.

- **Does the plan fit together?** It is vital that the elements of a business plan are consistent. Do the cash-flow forecasts and forecast profit or loss match the sales forecasts, and are they consistent with the results of market research?

Why start-ups can be risky
Revised

The risks facing a start-up business are all interdependent. Thus, for example, a threat to a business that originates in a change in the market (the emergence of a new competitor) can become a financial risk (falling sales revenue) very quickly.

Market-based risks

These can take a number of forms. There might be a change in the pattern of demand which leads to a decline in sales. In 2008 the UK's economy went into a deep recession. This caused extreme difficulties for small businesses selling products such as new houses, luxury holidays and jewellery.

Changes in the market can cause other problems for businesses. A fall in price of the product can ruin financial forecasts, while sales forecasts may be wildly inaccurate if a health scare occurs or a new and improved product enters the market. A new business may find difficulty in attracting sufficient customers. Even if its primary market research suggested that people would buy its products, it can be difficult persuading people to change suppliers.

Financial risks

The major financial risk for most new businesses is a shortage of funds — both short term and long term. New businesses may not have sufficient capital to, for example, find a suitable location for the business. In the case of retailers, this can pose a significant threat to the business's survival. Equally, cash shortages (possibly because customers are slow in paying) may mean that the start-up business cannot pay its own suppliers. Failure to meet their payment terms may result in the closure of the business. Banks may be unwilling to lend money to new businesses with a very limited trading record.

Operating risks

These can take a number of forms. Breakdowns, late deliveries, substandard supplies, unreliable employees, and safety or security problems can all prevent the production process taking place, or taking place in time to meet customer needs. These risks are much more real for a new business that does not have customer goodwill, experience or extra cash resources to help overcome the possible problems.

Why start-up businesses may fail
Revised

The reasons why start-up businesses are risky are also largely the reasons why they fail. A high proportion of start-up businesses do not survive the first few years of trading. Research has revealed that 53% of the businesses that started trading during 2003 were not trading in 2007.

The precise causes of failure vary according to the type of start-up business and its market. Nevertheless there are a number of common causes:

- **Lack of management skills and experience.** Many people who manage a start-up business have not done so before. They lack experience and may not recognise the signs of impending problems or, if they do, they may take inappropriate action or possibly no action. New managers may not be able to motivate employees or negotiate favourable deals with suppliers and customers. They may not have the necessary contacts in the business world to seek advice when things go badly.

- **Insufficient demand.** Market research is not always reliable and it is easy for entrepreneurs to interpret it positively when they are keen to get their new enterprise established. However, it is common for sales (perhaps after an initial boom) to be below expectations. This may force price cuts, which can threaten the business's survival.

- **Cash-flow problems.** Many managers are not aware of the importance of cash flow and of how difficult it can be to manage it successfully in a start-up business. Research has shown that cash-flow problems cause the failure of many start-up businesses.

- **Unexpected events.** The slowdown in spending in the economy due to the recession in 2008 led to an 8.5% rise in the number of small UK businesses failing. While not all of these were start-up businesses, it does indicate the impact that an unexpected event can have on the survival chances of vulnerable small businesses. Other unexpected events might include changes in tastes or fashions and the innovation of new products by competitors.

> **Now test yourself**
>
> 7 Following the recession of 2008 and slow growth up to 2011, the UK's economy is expected to continue to grow slowly and consumers will be cautious about spending money. Explain how this might create market risks, operating risks and financial risks for a retailer.
>
> Answers on p. 101
>
> Tested ☐

Tested ☐

Check your understanding

1 Define the term 'revenue'.
2 Define the term 'budget'.
3 State two examples of fixed costs and two examples of variable costs.
4 Complete the formula: contribution = sales revenue – ?
5 Complete the formula: fixed costs = total costs – ?
6 State the formula to calculate breakeven output.
7 If fixed costs rise, will a business have to produce and sell more or less to break even?
8 If a business increases its selling price, which line on its breakeven chart will move and in which direction?
9 If a business's opening balance in July is (£10,000) and its net cash flow is £7,500 for the month, what is its closing balance for July?
10 A business sells 150 products each month for £250 each. Its fixed costs are £1,200 monthly and the variable cost of each product is £90. Calculate its monthly profits.
11 A manufacturer faces annual fixed costs of £280,000. The selling price of its products is £240 and its variable costs are £140 per product. How many products does it need to produce and sell each year to break even?
12 A business sells 100,000 burgers each year for an average price of £2.50. The average variable cost of each burger is £1.90. Calculate the business's total contribution for the year.
13 Why should an entrepreneur forecast sales revenue as the first stage in the process of setting budgets?
14 Explain two weaknesses of using breakeven analysis as a technique of financial planning.

15 Why does an increase in price not always lead to an increase in a business's revenue?

16 Why is profit an important target for most businesses?

17 Explain two reasons why a start-up entrepreneur might draw up budgets for the first year of trading.

18 Explain the difference between market-based and operating risks as causes of business failure.

19 Explain two possible objectives an entrepreneur might have when starting a social enterprise.

20 Explain two reasons why cash-flow problems are a major reason for the failure of start-up businesses.

Answers on p. 101

Exam practice

Pip Collier has just completed his business plan in preparation for a meeting with his bank manager. He has applied for a bank loan of £150,000 which is 60% of the cost of starting his new ice-cream parlour in Great Yarmouth. He is about to give up a well-paid job as a teacher.

He has not started or managed a business before and has been advised to plan his cash flow carefully. However, Pip thinks that the most important part of his financial planning was drawing up his budgets to see if the business will make a profit.

His business plan shows that his monthly fixed costs will be £30,000 and he expects to sell his ice creams for an average price of £2.00 with average variable costs of £1.20.

Questions

a Define the term 'cash flow'.   [2]

b Calculate how many ice creams Pip will have to sell during his first year of trading if his business is to break even.   [6]

c Was drawing up budgets the most important part of Pip's financial planning? Justify your view.   [12]

Answers and quick quiz 4 online

Online

5 Finance

Using budgets

The benefits and drawbacks of using budgets
Revised

A **budget** is a financial plan. The detail of a budget should be the result of negotiation with all concerned. Those responsible for keeping to a budget should play a part in setting it, if it is to work as an effective motivator.

> **budget** — a financial plan

Benefits of budgets

Using budgets offers several benefits:

- Targets can be set for each part of a business, allowing managers to identify the extent to which each part contributes to the business's performance.
- Inefficiency and waste can be identified, so that appropriate remedial action can be taken.
- Budgets make managers think about the financial implications of their actions and focus decision making on the achievement of objectives.
- Budgeting should improve financial control by preventing overspending.
- Budgets can help improve internal communication.
- Delegated or devolved budgets can be used as a motivator by giving employees authority and the opportunity to fulfil some of their higher-level needs, as identified by Maslow (see pp. 64–65). At the same time, senior managers can retain control of the business by monitoring budgets.

> **Typical mistake**
>
> When answering questions on the benefits of budgets, students often write only about the use of budgets in preventing overspending. Make sure that you can argue a wider range of points.

Drawbacks of budgets

The use of budgets can have the following disadvantages:

- The operation of budgets can become inflexible. For example, sales may be lost if the marketing budget is followed when competitors implement major promotional campaigns.
- Budgets have to be accurate to have any meaning. Wide variances between budgeted and actual figures can demotivate staff and waste the resources used to prepare the budgets.

How to calculate and interpret variances
Revised

Variance analysis is the study by managers of the differences between planned activities in the form of budgets and the actual results that were achieved. Table 5.1 is an example of a monthly budget for a restaurant.

As the period covered by the budget unfolds, actual results can be compared with the budgeted figures and variances calculated and examined.

A **positive (or favourable) variance** occurs when costs are lower than forecast or profit or revenues higher, as in the case of sales revenue and profits in Table 5.1.

A **negative (or adverse) variance** arises when costs are higher than expected or revenues are less than anticipated. Examples include wage costs and food and drink in Table 5.1.

> **variance analysis** — the study by managers of the differences between planned activities in the form of budgets and the actual results that were achieved

Table 5.1 An example of calculating variances

Item	Budget figure (£)	Actual figure (£)	Variance (£)
Sales revenue	39,500	42,420	2,920 (favourable)
Fixed costs	9,500	9,500	0
Wages costs	10,450	11,005	555 (adverse)
Food and drink	8,475	9,826	1,351 (adverse)
Other costs	5,300	6,000	700 (adverse)
Total costs	33,725	36,331	2,606 (adverse)
Profit/loss	5,775	6,089	314 (favourable)

How to use variances to inform decision making

Revised

Positive variances might occur because of good budgetary control or by accident: for example, due to rising market prices.

Possible responses to positive variances are:

● to increase production if prices are rising, giving increased profit margins

● to reduce prices if costs are below expectations and the business aims to increase its sales

● to reinvest into the business or pay shareholders higher dividends if profits exceed expectations

Negative variances might occur because of inadequate control or factors outside the firm's control, such as rising raw material costs.

Possible responses to negative variances are:

● to reduce costs (e.g. by buying less expensive materials)

● to increase advertising in order to increase sales of the product and revenues

● to reduce prices to increase sales (relies on demand being price elastic)

The key issue about using the results of variance analysis to help decision making is to take into account the causes of the adverse or favourable variances. Just because a result is favourable does not mean that everything is in order. Neither does an adverse variance mean that the area responsible has been inefficient. A favourable production material variance could be generated from using lower-quality raw materials, which in turn could manifest itself as a drop in sales. Similarly, an adverse cost variance may occur because sales are higher than forecast and the business has incurred extra costs in supplying customers' demands.

> **Examiner's tip**
>
> Look for the relationships between revenues, costs and profits when considering variances. For example, if sales revenue has recorded a negative variance, it would be reasonable to expect costs, especially variable costs, to show a positive variance. If they do not, profits are likely to have a negative variance.

Now test yourself

1 Draw up a table to show four possible causes of favourable variances and four possible causes of adverse variances. For each cause of variance that you have listed, identify an appropriate response.

Answers on p. 101

Improving cash flow

The causes of cash-flow problems

There are several causes of cash-flow problems:

- **Poor management.** If managers do not forecast and monitor the business's cash flow, problems are more likely to arise and lead to a serious financial situation. Similarly, the failure to chase up customers who have not paid can lead to lower inflows and cash shortages.

- **Giving too much trade credit.** When a firm offers trade credit, it gives its customers time to settle their accounts — possibly 30, 60 or 90 days. This is an interest-free loan and while it may attract customers it slows the business's cash inflows, reducing its cash balance.

- **Overtrading.** This occurs when a business expands rapidly without planning how to finance the expansion. A growing business must pay for materials and labour before receiving the cash inflow from sales. It does this on an increasing scale and may struggle to fund its expenditure.

- **Unexpected expenditure.** A business may incur unexpected costs, resulting in a cash outflow. The breakdown of a machine can lead to significant outflows of cash, weakening the enterprise's cash position.

The methods of improving cash flow

There are a number of methods of improving cash flow.

Factoring

Factoring enables a business to sell its outstanding debtors to a specialist debt collector, called a factor. The business receives about 80% of the value of the debt immediately. The factor then receives payment from the customer and passes on the balance to the firm, holding back about 5% to cover expenses. This improves the business's cash-flow position as it does not have to wait for payment. Factoring does reduce profit margins, as approximately 5% of revenue is 'lost'.

Sale and leaseback

Here the owner of an asset (such as property) sells it and then leases it back. It provides a short-term boost to the business's finances, as the sale of the asset generates revenue. However, the business commits itself to paying rent to use the asset for the foreseeable future.

Improved working capital control

Working capital is the cash available to a business for its day-to-day operations. Working capital can be increased by:

- selling stocks of finished goods quickly, prompting cash inflows
- making customers pay on time and offering less trade credit (although this may damage sales)
- persuading suppliers to offer longer periods of trade credit, slowing cash outflows

Other possibilities are:

- stimulating sales, by offering discounts for cash and prompt payment
- selling off excess material stocks

> **working capital** — the cash available to a business for its day-to-day operations

> **Examiner's tip**
>
> Try to match the solution for cash-flow problems to their cause. This makes it much easier for you to justify your solution.

> **Now test yourself**
>
> 2 Draw up a two-column table to show four possible causes of cash-flow problems. In each case suggest an appropriate solution to the problem.
>
> **Answers on p. 102**
>
> Tested ☐

Measuring and increasing profit

How to calculate and understand profit margins — Revised ☐

Profit is the amount that is left over from revenue after all costs incurred in earning that revenue have been deducted. Profit is an objective for many, but not all, businesses. It is simplistic to say that a business that makes a larger profit than another business is performing better. It may be that the business with higher profits is larger. A profit figure is more meaningful if it is compared to something else.

The **net profit margin** is a ratio that calculates the business's profit after the deduction of all costs as a percentage of its revenue from sales.

> **profit** — the amount that is left over from revenue after all costs incurred in earning that revenue have been deducted

$$\text{net profit margin} = \frac{\text{net profit}}{\text{sales revenue}} \times 100$$

A business can calculate a profit margin for a single product or for all of its production. Table 5.2 shows examples of both of these methods of calculation.

Table 5.2 Net profit margin for a single product or for a business's entire output

Units sold	Sales revenue (£)	Total costs (£)	Profit (£)	Net profit margin (%)
24,500	232,750	200,165	32,585	14.0
1	9.50	8.17	1.33	14.0

Higher profit margins are generally better than lower ones. A higher profit margin can give a business a greater level of overall profit, assuming sales are constant. It allows a business to reward its owners more fully and/or to invest in improving its scale or efficiency.

> **Examiner's tip**
>
> Always show your workings when calculating a profit margin. If you make an arithmetical error, you will then still receive some of the marks available. If an examination paper includes a firm's profit margin, do not ignore it. Try to use it to develop an argument in answer to one of the questions.

Profit margins vary according to the type of business. Food retailers seek to sell food quickly and will accept a relatively low profit margin (Tesco plc's was 5.6% in 2011) because they sell a large volume of products. In contrast, other retailers that sell more expensive products less frequently seek a higher profit margin. A jeweller would expect a much higher profit margin than Tesco.

How to calculate and understand return on capital

Revised

Profits are the result of an investment by the business's owners. One way of judging the profitability of a business is to compare the amount of profit to the investment needed to start the enterprise or project.

The formula to calculate return on capital is:

$$\text{return on capital} = \frac{\text{net profit}}{\text{capital investment}} \times 100$$

Assume an entrepreneur sets up a business by investing £250,000, and in a given year the business generates a net profit of £12,500. The return on capital in these circumstances would be £12,500/£250,000 × 100 = 5%.

Again a higher figure is preferable. However, it is advisable to look at the return over a number of years. An expanding business will take time to develop a customer base and its return on capital may improve over time. Businesses with high returns on capital are frequently risky. It is wise to judge the return on capital against the degree of risk. Finally, take opportunity cost into account. In what other ways could this capital have been invested? A safer use with a slightly lower return might be a better use of the capital.

Methods of improving profits and profitability

Revised

Profitability measures profits against some yardstick, such as the sales revenue achieved by the business.

> **profitability** — measures profits against some yardstick, such as the sales revenue achieved by the business

Firms can increase their profits and/or profitability by taking a variety of actions:

- **Increasing prices.** An increase in price may increase revenue without raising total costs. However, this is a risk because an increase in price may cause a large fall in sales, leading to a reduction in profits if the fall in sales more than offsets the increase in price. The extent to which this happens depends upon price elasticity of demand (see pp. 89–90).
- **Cutting costs.** Lower costs of production can increase profit margins but possibly at the expense of quality. Reduced quality could reduce the volume of sales and the firm's reputation.
- **Using its capacity as fully as possible.** If a business has productive capacity that is not being utilised, its profits will be lower than they could be. If train companies run services that are only 50% occupied, their revenue is much lower. Offering incentives to customers to use

the trains could increase profits, as it costs little more to run a full train than a half-full one.

● **Increasing efficiency.** Avoiding waste in the form of poor quality and unsaleable products, using staff fully and using minimal resources to make products are all ways of improving the efficiency of a business. Improving efficiency is likely to result in increased profits.

The distinction between cash flow and profit   Revised

Cash flow and profit are very different concepts. Profit, at its simplest, is the surplus of revenues over total costs, over some time period. If a business earns revenues of £2 million during a financial year and incurs total costs of £1.5 million, it will generate profits of £0.5 million.

Cash flow relates to the timing of inflows and outflows of cash to and from a business. The profitable business referred to above might experience cash-flow problems for a variety of reasons. Those listed below are arguably the most important:

● **If its customers are slow to pay.** This delays its cash inflows and may lead to it having difficulty in settling its own bills as they fall due.

● **If it offers long periods of trade credit.** Giving customers 30 or 60 days to settle their accounts may help to increase sales but can result in a shortage of cash when needed.

Even profitable businesses may face difficulties if they do not manage their cash flow effectively.

> **Typical mistake**
>
> Many students use the terms 'profit' and 'cash' interchangeably but these terms have very different meanings. If a question asks you about cash flow, write only about cash flow, and for a question on profits or profitability avoid drifting into cash flow.

> **Now test yourself**
>
> 3 List four ways in which a business might increase its profit margin.
>
> 4 Explain three ways in which a business could increase its profits.
>
> **Answers on p. 102**
>
> Tested

Check your understanding   Tested

1 Define the term 'variance'.
2 State two examples of a favourable variance.
3 What is calculated using the following formula: net profit × 100/sales revenue?
4 Which is preferable, a 5% figure for return on capital employed (ROCE) or a 10% figure? Why?
5 What is the difference between profits and profitability?
6 Explain two ways in which an airline might improve its level of profits.
7 In what ways might a growing business benefit from the use of budgets?
8 How might a hotel respond to an adverse variance on its income budget?

Answers on p. 102

Exam practice

Piran Ltd sells wooden toys throughout the European Union — this is a competitive market with new firms entering it. The company has an excellent reputation for selling quality products and charges prices about 5% higher than those of its competitors. In recent months its profits have declined alarmingly and Pete Whyte, Piran Ltd's major shareholder, has cut costs, including 50% of the company's (already small) marketing budget.

Table 5.3 Piran Ltd's budget for August

Item	Budget £	Actual £	Variance £
Sales revenue	398,000	341,500	56,500 (adverse)
Fixed costs	45,000	44,950	50 (favourable)
Materials	194,575	189,000	5,575 (favourable)
Wages	78,210	77,025	1,185 (favourable)
Other costs	60,175	61,230	1,055 (adverse)
Total costs	377,960		

Pete has taken the decision to reduce the company's prices by 10% to increase sales and to restore the company's profits. His factory manager is more concerned about declining quality and that the percentage of toys returned has risen from 1% to 3.5% in one year.

Questions

a   Calculate Piran Ltd's profit variance for August.   [6]

b   Analyse the possible reasons why Piran Ltd may have recorded an adverse sales revenue variance in August.   [9]

c   Do you agree with Pete's decision to reduce prices to improve the company's profitability? Justify your decision.   [15]

Answers and quick quiz 5 online

Online

6 People in business

Improving organisational structures

The key elements of an organisational structure
Revised ☐

An organisational structure shows how roles in a particular enterprise are arranged to allow the business to perform its activities. This structure sets out the relationships between the different parts of the organisation, including its lines of communication and authority.

Levels of hierarchy

The **level of hierarchy** refers to the number of layers of authority in an organisation. In the past, many organisations were tall, with numerous layers of hierarchy, and were often authoritarian. Figure 6.1 shows an organisation with four levels of hierarchy. This is a 'flat' organisation.

> **level of hierarchy** — the number of layers of authority in an organisation
>
> **span of control** — the number of subordinates for whom a manager is directly responsible

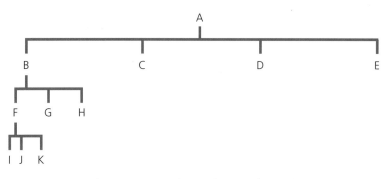

Figure 6.1 Hierarchies and spans of control

Spans of control

The **span of control** is the number of subordinates for whom a manager is directly responsible. In Figure 6.1, manager A has a span of control of 4 because he or she is not directly responsible for employees F, G, H, I, J and K. Employee B has a span of control of 3. The maximum recommended span for effective management is 6. The span of control used will depend upon:

- The experience and personality of the manager. Experienced managers might use wider spans.
- The nature of the business. If junior employees require a great deal of close supervision, a narrower span might be operated.
- The skills and attitudes of the employees. Highly skilled, professional employees might flourish in a business that adopts wide spans of control.

- The tradition of the organisation. A business with a tradition of democratic management and empowered workers may operate wider spans of control.

Workloads and job allocations

Workload refers to the number of duties that an employee is expected to carry out. It is cost effective for a business to ask employees to carry out the maximum amount of duties. Owners of small and medium-sized businesses often work long hours to make the enterprise succeed. They may expect employees to show a similar commitment and to work long hours. In some businesses, the workload may vary according to the time of year: the workloads of agricultural workers are likely to be higher in the summer months, for example.

Job allocation is a term used to describe the way in which the organisation's duties are divided among the different employees in the business. In a small business, it is normal for employees to carry out a wide range of duties. This may be because the business cannot afford to hire specialist staff to carry out certain tasks. As a business grows, it may hire specialist employees and the job allocations of individual employees may become less varied.

> **workload** — the number of duties that an employee is expected to carry out
>
> **job allocation** — the way in which the organisation's duties are divided among the different employees in the business
>
> **delegation** — the passing of authority to a subordinate within the organisation
>
> **authority** — the power to carry out the task

Delegation

Delegation is the passing of authority to a subordinate within the organisation. Although a task may be passed down from a superior to a subordinate, the manager still has responsibility for ensuring that the job is completed. **Authority** is the power to carry out the task. It is possible to delegate authority, but responsibility remains with the delegator.

To delegate, a manager must trust the delegatee and it is important that the subordinate feels that trust is placed in them. A prudent manager will also want to exercise some control over the subordinate via reports and inspections, for example. Any increase in control exercised by the manager decreases the amount of trust enjoyed by the subordinate. The use of delegation has implications for the workloads of both parties involved.

> **Typical mistake**
>
> Students often refer to 'responsibility being passed down the organisational structure'. This is not the case. It is authority that is passed down.

Communication flows

Communication is the exchange of information or ideas between two or more parties. For a business to operate effectively, it is important that effective communication takes place throughout the organisation.

> **communication** — the exchange of information or ideas between two or more parties

Figure 6.2 shows that communication flows can be:

- upward (from junior to more senior employees)
- sideways or horizontal (between employees in the same level of hierarchy of the organisation)
- downwards from senior to junior employees

Communication should be two-way. This enables the sender of the communication to confirm that the message has been understood and the recipient to raise any necessary queries.

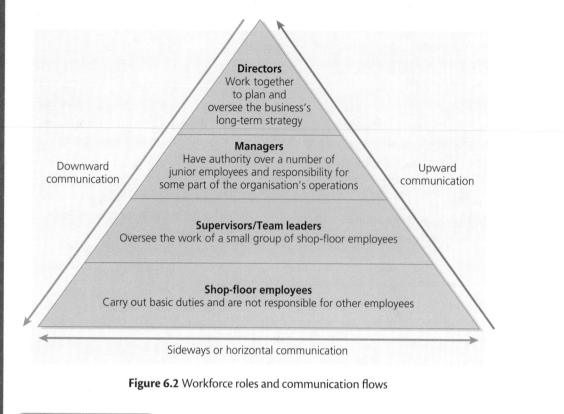

Figure 6.2 Workforce roles and communication flows

Workforce roles

Revised ☐

A workforce comprises employees whose roles can be categorised in a number of ways. One possible classification is set out below.

- **Shop-floor employees.** Shop-floor employees carry out basic duties in an organisation. One example is clerks in an office. They are at the bottom of the organisational structure and are not responsible for other employees.

- **Supervisors or team leaders.** Supervisors provide a link between managers and shop-floor workers, and have responsibility for other employees. They may also have the authority to take certain decisions on routine issues such as staff rotas. Team leaders carry out a similar role, but they may work alongside shop-floor workers.

- **Managers.** Managers are responsible for organising others in the business and possibly for a certain part of the business. Managers have to plan, organise, motivate and control.

- **Directors.** Directors are elected by the shareholders of the company and work together as a team: the board of directors. The directors set out the main aims of the business and monitor the strategies that the business adopts to try to meet its aims. Full-time or executive directors are responsible for important elements within the business such as marketing. Part-time or non-executive directors normally bring some particular expertise to the business.

Organisational structure and business performance

Revised ☐

Small and medium-sized businesses seek an organisational structure that allows them to:

- operate as efficiently as possible
- operate flexibly as the enterprise grows and changes

An efficient organisational structure can help a business to use its human resources effectively. Using employees efficiently means that they should have a manageable workload and this should encourage high levels of motivation and productivity. In service industries such as catering, this can result in high levels of customer service. The organisation should also be structured to employ people in ways that allow them to use their skills. These skills might relate to a function, such as finance or marketing, or relate to more generic management duties.

An organisational structure is likely to change over time, particularly if a business is growing. Creating more levels of hierarchy or appointing more people at particular levels in the hierarchy can help the organisation to be responsive and prevent people overworking. If managers are aware of the relationships between the organisation's structure and its performance, it is likely that they will allow the structure to evolve to provide a responsive and efficient service to customers.

> **Examiner's tip**
>
> Answers in this area frequently reveal a lack of understanding about the relationship between organisational structure and business performance. It can be a complex topic and is one on which you should spend time.

Now test yourself

Tested ☐

1 Make a list of the circumstances in which a business can (i) operate wide spans of control whilst managing employees effectively and (ii) only operate effectively by using narrow spans of control.

Answers on p. 102

The effectiveness of the workforce

Measuring the effectiveness of the workforce

Revised ☐

Managers need to measure employee performance objectively to:

● assess the efficiency (and competitiveness) of the workforce

● assist in developing the workforce plan

● confirm that the business's human resource planning is working effectively

Monitoring the performance of employees helps to identify the need for training, further recruitment, redundancy or redeployment. There are two major ways in which a business can assess the performance of its labour force.

Labour productivity

$$\text{labour productivity} = \frac{\text{output per period}}{\text{number of employees at work}} \times 100$$

If employees produce a similar or greater quantity than employees of rival businesses per time period then productivity may be satisfactory. However, such comparisons are simplistic: wage rates, the level of technology and the way the labour force is organised also affect productivity.

Labour turnover

$$\text{labour turnover (\%)} = \frac{\text{number of staff leaving during the year}}{\text{average number of staff}} \times 100$$

Labour turnover is the proportion of a business's staff leaving their employment over a period of time. A high level of labour turnover could be caused by many factors:

- inadequate wage levels, leading employees to defect to competitors
- poor morale and low levels of motivation within the workforce
- the selection of the wrong employees, meaning they leave to seek more suitable employment
- a buoyant local labour market, offering more attractive opportunities to employees

> **labour turnover** — the proportion of a business's staff leaving their employment

> **Typical mistake**
>
> It is important to express answers to calculations in the correct format. When calculating productivity, for example, many students express their answers as percentages and not as a number of units of output per time period.

How to interpret the results
Revised

Higher rates of productivity are preferable to lower rates. Higher rates can, in effect, reduce the costs of production, allowing a business to charge lower prices or to enjoy higher profit margins. However, if high levels of productivity are achieved at the expense of quality and customer satisfaction, gains may exist only in the short term.

Lower rates of labour turnover are also preferable, although some turnover is essential to bring fresh ideas, skills and enthusiasm into the workforce. High rates are expensive in terms of additional recruitment costs, lost production and the damage to morale and productivity.

> **Examiner's tip**
>
> It is important to look behind any labour force data that are provided. For example, two sets of productivity data may suggest that firm A has a clear advantage. This may become less clear cut when the following factors relating to firm B are taken into account:
> - wage rates are significantly lower
> - morale is excellent
> - a training programme is being implemented, causing short-term disruption
> - there is a low incidence of industrial relations problems
> - a reputation for craftsmanship and quality products has been established

Developing an effective workforce

The recruitment process
Revised

Recruitment is finding and appointing new employees. All businesses, even small ones, need to recruit employees at some stage. The recruitment process is shown in Figure 6.3.

> **recruitment** — finding and appointing new employees

Recruitment documentation

The necessary documentation for the recruitment process is shown below.

Job adverts normally contain the job title, a description of duties, the location of the workplace and possibly salary and working hours.

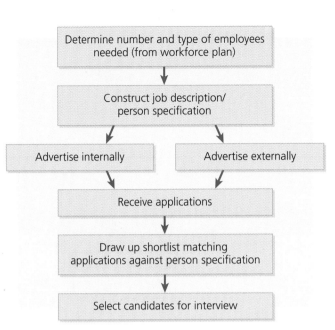

Figure 6.3 The process of recruitment

The advert may be local for a relatively unskilled job. Highly skilled and professional positions might require advertising nationally or even internationally.

Job descriptions set out the duties and tasks associated with a particular post. They may act as the basis for preparing the job advert and relate to the position rather than the person. Typically, job descriptions contain the following information:

- title of the post
- employment conditions
- some idea of tasks and duties
- to whom employees are responsible
- likely targets and standards that employees are expected to meet

Person or job specifications set out the qualifications and qualities required of an employee. The specification might include:

- educational and professional qualifications required
- character and personality traits expected
- physical characteristics needed
- experience necessary

Recruitment can be an expensive exercise but is less costly than appointing the wrong employee and having to repeat the process.

> **job descriptions** — set out the duties and tasks associated with a particular post
>
> **person or job specifications** — set out the qualifications and qualities required of an employee

Internal and external recruitment

Revised

Recruitment may take place either internally or externally.

Internal recruitment

Firms may recruit internally through promotion or by redeploying existing employees. This offers several benefits:

- It is cheaper, as it avoids the need for expensive external advertising.

- Candidates will have experience of the business and may not require induction training.
- Selection may be easier, as more is known about the candidates.

However, problems exist in recruiting internally:

- Selection is from a smaller pool of available labour and the calibre of candidates may be lower. This can be a problem for senior appointments.
- Difficulties can result if employees are promoted from within as some employees may resent taking orders from those they previously worked alongside.

External recruitment

The advantages of this approach are:

- It is probable that higher-quality candidates will be available, even if advertisements are only placed in local media.
- External candidates will bring fresh ideas and enthusiasm into the business.

But again, drawbacks exist:

- It is more expensive to recruit externally using national advertising or employment agencies.
- The degree of risk is greater as candidates are less well known to the business.

> **Typical mistake**
>
> Students sometimes provide huge amounts of information on recruitment and selection. This is primarily a descriptive area and one on which relatively straightforward questions testing knowledge are normally set. Few marks are normally available for such questions. It is more important to appreciate the role of recruitment and selection within the whole human resource management process and the influences on this process.

Selecting the best employees   Revised ☐

Selection is the choice of one or more employees from amongst those who have applied for jobs with a business. Because it is costly to appoint the wrong people, businesses are investing more resources into the recruitment and selection process.

> **selection** — the choice of one or more employees from amongst those who have applied for jobs with a business

A range of selection techniques exist:

- **Interviews** remain the most common form of selection and may involve varying numbers of interviewers. They are relatively cheap and allow the two-way exchange of information, but are unreliable for selection. Some people perform well at interview, but that does not necessarily mean they will perform well in the post.
- **Psychometric tests** reveal more about the personality of a candidate than might be discovered through interview. Questions are frequently used to assess candidates' management skills or their ability to work in a team.
- **Aptitude tests** may provide an insight into a candidate's current ability and potential. Such tests can also be used to assess intelligence and job-related skills.
- **Assessment centres** involve a number of methods of selection, including role-plays and group activities. Assessment centres allow a direct comparison to be made between candidates.

How recruitment and selection improve a workforce

Appointing the wrong people can be very costly. Firstly, they may make errors when carrying out their work (e.g. supplying the wrong products to particular customers), leading to lost sales and reduced profits. In a highly competitive market, or for a business that is seeking growth, recruiting the wrong people can make it difficult for a business to achieve its objectives.

Secondly, recruitment is an expensive process. Costs are incurred in advertising as well as in staff time spent selecting people to be interviewed and during the selection stage. As senior employees may be involved in the selection process, the labour costs can be high. A survey by *Personnel Today* revealed that recruitment costs, excluding advertising, exceed £5,000 per employee.

However, recruiting the right people to a business offers benefits:

- Levels of productivity are likely to be high, improving the business's financial performance.
- If people are in the right job, they have the skills to make a greater contribution to the business.
- Effective recruitment reduces the workload of line managers, freeing them for other duties.
- Effective recruitment saves time in disciplining, dismissing and replacing people who do not perform well.

> **Examiner's tip**
>
> High-scoring answers in the area of recruitment and selection frequently link this topic to others in the AQA AS specification. You may be able to develop answers by referring to quality, minimising costs and customer loyalty.

Methods of training

Training is the provision of job-related skills and knowledge. Almost all employees receive some training when they commence a particular job. This is known as **induction training**. Induction training is intended to introduce an employee to the business in which they will be working. It may include familiarisation with some or all of the following:

> **training** — the provision of job-related skills and knowledge

- policies and procedures, such as appraisal, holiday entitlement, and discipline and grievance
- personnel with whom the new employee will be working
- health and safety and security procedures
- the fundamental duties associated with the job

Induction training offers a number of advantages to businesses:

- it enables a new recruit to become more productive more quickly
- it can prevent costly errors resulting from employee ignorance
- it may make a new employee feel more welcome and reduce labour turnover

There are two broad types of training:

- **Off-the-job.** This is training outside the workplace, at a college or some other training agency, or at the employee's home. Off-the-job training may be external courses comprising lectures and seminars, self-study or open learning.
- **On-the-job.** This type of training is carried out in the workplace. The trainee learns from more experienced employees through observation

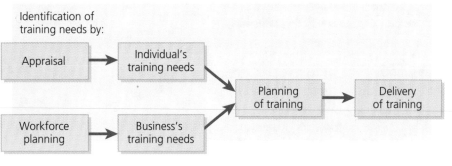

Figure 6.4 Training

and work shadowing. Alternatively, the trainee may work through instruction manuals, operate with a mentor or receive more formal guidance from senior employees.

The advantages and disadvantages of each type of training are shown in Table 6.1.

Table 6.1 Advantages and disadvantages of training

	Off-the-job	On-the-job
Advantages	• Employees are not distracted by work pressures. • Specialists can be used to provide training. • Often carries greater conviction with employees.	• Simple to organise and often relatively cheap. • Closely related to the needs and circumstances of the business. • Employees can see the relevance of the training.
Disadvantages	• Can be costly. • Employees absent from work for a period of time. • Can place greater pressures (extra hours, commitment) on other employees. • If general training, employees may leave when complete.	• Those delivering training often do not have teaching or training skills. • Trainees can be distracted by the demands of the job (e.g. by phone calls). • Training can be narrowly focused, not looking at the broader needs of the organisation.

In spite of being expensive and disruptive, training does offer organisations a number of benefits:

● Well-trained employees will be better motivated, as they feel valued and get a sense of achievement from performing their work more efficiently or carrying out more complex duties.

● Training improves employee performance, resulting in a more productive and efficient workforce. This can improve the competitiveness of the organisation.

● Training can help to reduce labour turnover, as employees are more satisfied with their work. It may also help to make the business more attractive to potential employees.

The government encourages training through its 'Investors in People' scheme. Firms that meet the requirement for training are entitled to use a logo identifying them as meeting the Investors in People standard. This may assist the business in its dealings with customers and other businesses. Indeed, some firms will only deal with suppliers if they have the Investors in People award.

Now test yourself

2 Write a list of the circumstances in which it would be best to use (i) internal recruitment and (ii) external recruitment.

3 Draw a mind map to show the ways in which the topic of recruitment and selection can be linked to other topic areas from the AQA AS specification.

4 Use Table 6.1 as a guide to draw up a table setting out the advantages and disadvantages of training employees.

Answers on p. 102

Motivating employees.

Theories of motivation

Revised

What is motivation?

Motivation is the range of factors that influence people to behave in certain ways. Analysts disagree on the precise meaning of the term 'motivation'. Some writers believe motivation is the will to work due to enjoyment of the work itself. This suggests that motivation comes from within an employee. An alternative view is that it is the will or desire to achieve a given target or goal, due to some external stimulus. Many of the differences in the theories of motivation can be explained in terms of this fundamental difference of definition. Figure 6.5 shows the various schools of thought relating to motivation.

> **motivation** — the range of factors that influence people to behave in certain ways

Examiner's tip

You don't need to know any particular theory of motivation. However, you should know at least one theory of financial methods of motivation and one theory of non-financial methods of motivation.

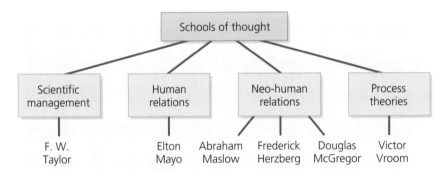

Figure 6.5 Schools of thought relating to motivation

The school of scientific management

A 'school of thought' is simply a group of people who hold broadly similar views. The school of scientific management argues that business decisions should be taken on the basis of data that are researched and tested quantitatively. Members of the school believe that it is vital to identify ways in which costs can be assessed and reduced, thus increasing efficiency. This school of thought supports the use of techniques such as work-study.

A member of the school of scientific management is **F. W. Taylor** (1856–1915). Taylor was a highly successful engineer who began to advise and lecture on management practices and was a consultant to Henry Ford. His theories were based on a simple interpretation of human behaviour.

Taylor's ideas were formulated during his time at the Bethlehem Steel Company in the USA. He believed in firm management based on scientific principles. He used a stopwatch to measure how long various activities took and sought the most efficient methods. He then detailed 'normal' times in which duties should be completed, and assessed individual performance against these. Efficiency, he argued, would improve productivity, competitiveness and profits. This required employees to be organised, closely supervised and paid according to how much they produced.

Taylor believed that people were solely motivated by money. Workers should have no control over their work and the social aspect of employment was considered irrelevant and ignored.

Taylor's views were unpopular with shop-floor employees. As workers and managers became more highly educated, they sought other ways of motivating and organising employees.

The human relations school of management

A weakness of the scientific school was that its work ignored the social needs of employees. This, and the obvious unpopularity of the ideas, led to the development of the human relations school. This school of thought concentrated on the sociological aspects of work.

A key writer was **Elton Mayo**. He is best remembered for his Hawthorne Studies at the Western Electric Company in Chicago between 1927 and 1932. He conducted experiments to discover whether employee performance was affected by factors such as breaks and the level of lighting. The results surprised Mayo. The productivity of one group of female employees increased both when the lighting was lessened and when it was increased. It became apparent that they were responding to the level of attention they were receiving. From this experiment, Mayo concluded that motivation depends on:

- the type of job being carried out and the type of supervision given to the employee
- group relationships, group morale and individuals' sense of worth

Mayo's work took forward the debate on management in general and motivation in particular. He moved the focus on to the needs of employees, rather than just the needs of the organisation. Although Mayo's research is nearly 80 years old, it still has relevance to modern businesses.

The neo-human relations school

Abraham Maslow and **Frederick Herzberg** are recognised as key members of this school of thought. While the human relations school associated with Elton Mayo highlighted the *sociological* aspects of work, the neo-human relations school considered the *psychological* aspects of employment.

Abraham Maslow

Abraham Maslow was an American psychologist who formulated a famous hierarchy of needs (Figure 6.6). According to Maslow, human needs consist of five types that form a hierarchy:

1 Physiological — the need for food, shelter, water and sex.

2 Security — the need to be free from threats and danger.

3 Social — the need to love and be loved, and to be part of a group.

4 Esteem — the need to have self-respect and the respect of colleagues.

5 Self-actualisation — the need to develop personal skills and fulfil one's potential.

Maslow argued that all individuals have a hierarchy of needs and that once one level of needs is satisfied, people can be motivated by tasks that offer the opportunity to satisfy the next level of needs.

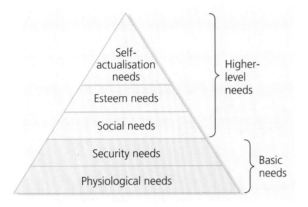

Figure 6.6 Maslow's hierarchy of needs

Some writers doubt the existence of a hierarchy of needs. They argue that social needs and esteem needs may coexist and that people do not move smoothly up a hierarchy, as Maslow's model suggests. However, his work brings psychology into motivational theory and highlights the range of individual needs that may be met through employment.

Frederick Herzberg

The research carried out by Frederick Herzberg offered some support for Maslow's views and focused on the psychological aspects of motivation. Herzberg asked 203 accountants and engineers to identify those factors about their employment that pleased and displeased them. Figure 6.7 summarises Herzberg's findings.

This research was the basis of Herzberg's two-factor theory, published in 1968. Herzberg divided the factors motivating people at work into two groups:

- **Motivators.** These are positive factors that give people job satisfaction (e.g. receiving recognition for effort) and therefore increase productivity as motivation rises.

- **Hygiene (or maintenance) factors.** These are factors that may cause dissatisfaction among employees. Herzberg argued that motivators should be built into the hygiene factors. Improving hygiene factors will not positively motivate but will reduce employee dissatisfaction. Examples of hygiene factors are pay, fair treatment and reasonable working conditions.

Herzberg did not argue that hygiene factors are unimportant. On the contrary, he contended that only when such factors are properly met can motivators begin to operate positively.

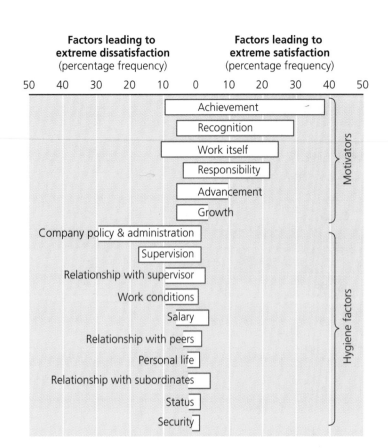

Figure 6.7 Herzberg's factors causing satisfaction and dissatisfaction

Process theories of motivation

The foremost writer on process theory is **Victor Vroom**, who published *Work and Motivation* in 1964. Vroom's theory expressed the view that motivation depends on people's expectations of the outcome. If working life offers opportunities for workers' expectations to be met, motivation is likely to be high. If the outcome of their actions is expected to be desirable, they will be motivated. The stronger the desire for the outcome, the greater is the level of motivation.

The use of financial methods to motivate employees

Revised ☐

Some writers, such as Herzberg, believe that money is not a positive motivator, although the lack of it can demotivate. Nevertheless, pay systems are designed to motivate employees financially.

Piece-rate pay

Piece-rate pay gives a payment for each item produced. This system encourages effort, but often at the expense of quality. Piece rate is common in agriculture and the textile industry.

Commission

Commission is a payment made to employees based on the value of sales achieved. It can form all or part of a salary package.

Profit-related pay

Profit-related pay gives employees a share of the profits earned by the business. It encourages all employees to work hard to generate the maximum profits for the business. It also offers some flexibility: in a recession, wages can fall with profits, reducing the need for redundancies.

Performance-related pay

Performance-related pay is used in many industries, from banking to education. It needs to be tied into some assessment or appraisal of employee performance. Whatever criteria are used to decide who should receive higher pay, the effect can be divisive and damaging to employee morale.

Share ownership

Employees are sometimes offered shares in the company in which they work. Shares can be purchased through savings schemes. However, share ownership may cause discontentment if this perk is available only to the senior staff.

> **Examiner's tip**
>
> Do consider the financial position of the business (in terms of profits and cash flow) when developing arguments in support of and against financial methods of motivation. There is likely to be numerical evidence in a case study if such a question has been asked.

Improving job design Revised

Many theorists have argued that jobs need to be designed with motivational factors in mind. They should not be too highly specialised and should offer varied duties. Equally, jobs need to allow employees to use their initiative and to meet social needs by working with others.

Modern-day managers have realised that money is not a great motivator and financial incentive schemes are difficult to operate. Teamworking may also mean that individual financial incentive schemes are inappropriate. Numerous non-financial methods of motivation have been developed.

Job enlargement

Job enlargement is extending an employee's range of duties to include extra, similar duties. This technique gives employees a broader workload of a similar nature. This gives a wider variety of tasks and lessens the repetition and monotony that are all too common on production lines. Job enlargement may offer advantages in the short term. This is also called **horizontal loading**.

> **job enlargement** — extending an employee's range of duties to include extra, similar duties

Job rotation

Job rotation is the regular switching of employees between tasks of a similar degree of complexity. Job rotation widens the activities of a worker by switching him or her around a range of work. For example, it may require an employee in an office to move regularly between staffing reception and inputting data on to a database. Job rotation offers the advantage of making it easier to cover for absent colleagues, but it may reduce productivity as workers are unfamiliar with new tasks.

> **job rotation** — the regular switching of employees between tasks of a similar degree of complexity

Job enrichment

Job enrichment is redesigning a job to include more challenging tasks. Job enrichment attempts to give employees greater responsibility by increasing the range and complexity of tasks they undertake and giving them the necessary authority. It motivates by giving employees the opportunity to use their abilities to the fullest. Herzberg argued that job enrichment should be a central element in any policy of motivation. According to Herzberg, enriched jobs should contain a range of tasks and challenges at different ability levels, and clear opportunities for achievement and feedback on performance. Job enrichment necessitates training.

> **job enrichment** — redesigning a job to include more challenging tasks

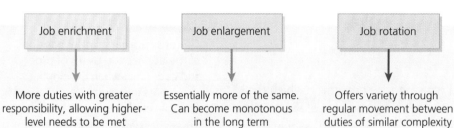

Figure 6.8 Job enrichment, enlargement and rotation

Team working and empowerment   Revised ☐

Empowerment

Empowerment involves giving people control over their working lives. This can be achieved by organising the labour force into teams with a high degree of autonomy. This approach to management derives from Mayo's work. Empowerment means that employees plan their own work, take their own decisions and solve their own problems. Teams are set targets to achieve and may receive rewards for doing so. Empowered teams motivate by allowing people the opportunity to meet some of the higher needs identified by Maslow or Herzberg's motivators.

> **empowerment** — giving people control over their working lives

Quality circles

Quality circles are small groups of fewer than 20 people who meet regularly to discuss and solve production problems. They allow employees an opportunity to contribute to decision making. Members are usually drawn from all levels within the organisation. This ensures all perspectives are considered. As well as motivating staff, groups can provide businesses with valuable ideas.

> **Examiner's tip**
>
> This is a common topic for examination questions, as empowered teams are a popular method of organising labour forces. It is important to appreciate the advantages and disadvantages of this approach. The advantages centre on the positive motivational effects. This can result in higher productivity, leading to improved competitiveness and higher profits or market share. Disadvantages (which may only exist in the short term) centre on the cost and disruption of training, and opposition from some employees.

Now test yourself   Tested ☐

5 Prepare a list of the theories of motivation that suggest that motivation is the result of some external stimuli and a list of those theories that suggest that motivation comes from within an individual employee. Has the view changed over time and which do you think is correct? Why?

6 Draw a mind map to link the major theories of motivation with the techniques of motivation that the writers might have recommended for use in the workplace.

Answers on p. 102

Check your understanding

1 Define the term 'span of control'.
2 Define the term 'level of hierarchy'.
3 Distinguish between delegation and authority.
4 What is the difference between a team leader and a supervisor?
5 Distinguish between a job description and a person specification.
6 State two benefits of training.
7 Explain two views on the meaning of motivation.
8 State the two formulae needed to calculate labour productivity and labour turnover.
9 Explain why a business might prefer to use external recruitment when appointing a new chief executive.
10 Explain why Elton Mayo would support the use of teams in the workplace.
11 A business has an average of 250 employees and 50 leave during the year. Calculate its labour turnover.
12 Explain the actions the business in Question 11 might take to reduce its labour turnover.
13 Explain two ways in which an effective system of recruitment and selection might improve the performance of a business's workforce.
14 Explain two reasons why a business might empower its employees.
15 Explain why a manager may decide not to use financial methods of motivation.

Answers on p. 103

Exam practice

Ian Higgs has owned and managed Timberlake Sheds Ltd since 1999. It manufactures a range of garden sheds. The company's financial performance has declined steadily and last year it made a small loss. The company's customers have complained about poor quality and poor customer service.

Last year his employees manufactured 14,000 sheds. The previous year the figure was 15,000 sheds. The size of the company's workforce has remained unchanged at 50 employees (with zero labour turnover) partly because they are relatively well paid.

Ian is not happy with the performance of his workforce and is considering how to improve this. He has decided to invest £2 million in training his company's shop-floor employees, but will not train its managers.

His other major plan is to implement a piece-rate system of payment for those employees working on its production line. This will also be linked to meeting quality targets.

Questions

a Calculate the change in the productivity level of the company's employees. [6]
b Analyse the benefits the company may receive from investing £2 million in training its employees. [9]
c Do you agree that Ian was correct to use financial methods of motivation? Justify your decision. [15]

Answers and quick quiz 6 online

7 Operations management

Making operational decisions

Operational targets Revised

Businesses may have three different types of operational target:

- unit costs
- quality targets
- capacity utilisation targets

Unit costs

Unit costs are the cost of producing a single, average unit of output. This may be either a good or a service. Unit costs are calculated by:

$$\text{unit costs} = \frac{\text{total costs}}{\text{units of output}}$$

For example, if a passenger ferry has 120 passengers and the total cost of one journey is £2,400, the unit cost of carrying a single passenger is £20. Businesses seek to reduce their unit costs, subject to meeting customers' needs in terms of quality.

Quality targets

Quality is meeting the needs of a customer. Businesses may set quality targets in terms of:

- having only a low percentage of faulty products, or possibly no faults — known as 'zero defects'
- reducing the number of customer complaints to a specified level
- achieving certain targets for customer satisfaction (as measured through market research)

Capacity utilisation

Capacity utilisation measures the extent to which a business uses the production resources that are available to it. The passenger ferry mentioned above may be able to carry 200 people on a single journey, but if it only carries 100 passengers, it is only using 50% of its resources or capacity. By increasing capacity utilisation, it is possible to increase revenue with only a relatively small increase in costs. We consider capacity utilisation more fully below.

> **unit cost** — the cost of producing a single, average unit of output
>
> **quality** — meeting the needs of a customer
>
> **capacity utilisation** — the extent to which a business uses the production resources that are available to it

Calculating and managing capacity utilisation Revised

What is capacity?

A **firm's capacity** is the maximum amount that the firm is physically capable of producing if it uses its available resources to their fullest extent.

Over time, a firm is likely to adjust its capacity to meet the demands of the marketplace. The following factors may affect the amount of capacity a business requires:

- the entry (or departure) of a competitor to (or from) the market
- a change in tastes or fashions, meaning higher or lower demand for the product
- new developments in products or new production techniques

A firm may adjust capacity by:

- investing in a completely new factory, shop or office, or extending an existing one
- closing down premises permanently
- closing down premises temporarily ('mothballing')

What is capacity utilisation?

Capacity utilisation measures the extent to which a business uses the production resources that are available to it. It can be measured using the formula:

$$\text{capacity utilisation (\%)} = \frac{\text{current output per month}}{\text{maximum output per month}} \times 100$$

Managing capacity utilisation

If a business under-utilises its capacity, it is said to have **spare** or **excess capacity**. Many of the consequences of this are unfavourable:

- the business is likely to face higher unit costs, as fixed costs are spread over fewer units of output
- profits and competitiveness may decline, since the firm is likely to charge higher prices
- labour and other resources may be idle, thereby reducing motivation
- the firm might produce more output than it can sell, leading to increased storage costs and possibly lower selling prices
- it may be necessary to lay off staff, adversely affecting the business's corporate image

Many businesses implement strategies to avoid having spare or unutilised capacity. There are two broad options:

- **Increase sales to use up the available capacity.** Entering new markets might achieve this — perhaps overseas, or by finding new uses for an existing product.
- **Reduce the capacity available to the firm.** This is known as rationalisation. It may mean selling land and buildings and other fixed assets and making staff redundant. This can be an unattractive and expensive option. Many firms may lease out spare capacity, transferring employees to other jobs if possible.

A business might face circumstances in which it has insufficient capacity and cannot meet demand for its products. In such a situation it has two options:

- Increase capacity by purchasing more fixed assets such as factories and machinery. This is likely to be expensive and time consuming.

> **firm's capacity** — the maximum amount that the firm is physically capable of producing if it uses its available resources to their fullest extent

Examiner's tip

To be able to write effectively on operations issues, as on many other topics, you should appreciate the circumstances in which the techniques might be employed. For example, a firm facing a short-term decline in the sales of its products may mothball a factory during a slump.

Typical mistake

It is important to express answers to calculations in the correct format. When calculating capacity utilisation, for example, many students express their answers as levels of production and not percentages.

Examiner's tip

Be clear about the benefits of high capacity utilisation and the methods of eliminating spare capacity and when they might be effective. Questions will require you to apply this knowledge to particular circumstances, so you should use your knowledge selectively.

- Subcontract production by finding a supplier to manufacture or supply part or all of the good or service. This is cheaper and quicker than increasing capacity.

The decision depends upon a range of factors, including whether the firm believes that the increase in demand will last. If so, it is more likely to increase its productive capacity permanently.

Operational issues: non-standard orders

Revised

Non-standard orders occur when a customer asks for products that do not meet the normal specifications for that supplier. For example, a supermarket may ask for products to be supplied in smaller containers.

Meeting this order would involve a number of operational issues:

- the use of a different range of cans and/or boxes
- adjustment of the business's packaging equipment before and after the order
- these changes are likely to lead to delays on the production line
- the operational costs of supplying this order are likely to be greater

Should the business accept the order? The answer depends on how important this customer is. A business that is seeking to expand may also accept the order as a means of increasing sales and market share, so long as it does not damage its profits.

Operational issues: matching supply and demand

Revised

This is a problem for businesses that face seasonal patterns of demand. Businesses such as fruit farms and some hotels face difficulties in matching the amount they supply with the volume that customers wish to purchase. This is a matter of managing capacity effectively. Managers can aim to increase capacity at certain times of the year, or possibly seek alternative uses for spare capacity when demand is low.

> **Now test yourself**
>
> 1 Make a list of the circumstances in which it is best for a business to eliminate spare capacity by (i) rationalisation and (ii) increasing sales.
>
> **Answers on p. 103**
>
> Tested

Effective operations: quality

The meaning of quality

Revised

A quality product meets customers' needs fully. Quality is a major determinant of a business's competitiveness.

If a firm produces poor quality products, it incurs:

- the costs of scrapping or re-working products
- additional costs if customers return goods for repair under warranty
- costs resulting from damage to the business's reputation

> **Examiner's tip**
>
> Remember that a quality product does not need to be a costly or premium product, so supplying quality products does not inevitably involve increased costs. Supplying quality products may increase revenue but have little impact on costs.

Quality can be important to businesses because:

- it can provide a USP, helping small firms to compete against large rivals
- it can allow businesses to charge higher prices, increasing profit margins
- it can enable a business to increase its sales

Quality control versus quality assurance

Revised

There is an important distinction between quality control and quality assurance.

Quality control

Quality control is the process of checking that completed production meets agreed criteria. Quality control inspectors usually undertake this task. However, quality control only identifies problems once the production process is complete. Quality control also aims to improve product design and includes the regular review of quality control procedures.

> **quality control** — the process of checking that completed production meets agreed criteria
>
> **quality assurance** — ensures that quality standards are attained by all employees in a business

Quality assurance

Quality assurance is implemented to ensure that quality standards are attained by all employees in a business. The aim is to maximise customer satisfaction, sales and profits. This policy affects all activities in the organisation and is intended to prevent problems, such as defective products, from occurring in the first place.

> **Typical mistake**
>
> It is important to use terms accurately. Many students write quality assurance when they mean quality control and vice versa, or use the terms interchangeably.

Systems of quality assurance

Revised

There are a number of different systems of quality assurance, of which **total quality management (TQM)** is probably the best known. TQM instils a culture of quality throughout the organisation. It places on all employees of a firm an individual and collective responsibility for maintaining high quality standards. It aims for prevention with a target of zero defects (see Figure 7.1).

> **TQM** — a culture of quality throughout the organisation

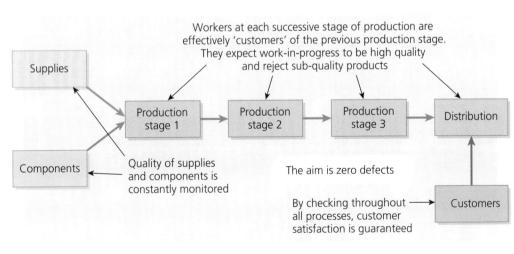

Figure 7.1 Total quality management

TQM has both an internal and an external dimension. Externally, the success of a firm depends on its ability to satisfy customers' demands. Product quality is likely to be a way in which a company can achieve a competitive advantage.

Internally, each department in a firm is viewed as a customer and/or a supplier. The firm has to meet consistently high standards in this 'internal' trading. Workers at each stage of the production process examine critically the work-in-progress they receive. Errors and faults are identified and rectified as soon as possible and customer satisfaction is assured.

Quality assurance systems are unlikely to succeed without the support of all employees. TQM seeks commitment to the highest quality standards in each of the internal stages of production. It minimises the time and money spent on quality by preventing quality problems. Employees' commitment to quality can be supported by the operation of quality circles (see p. 68).

Examiner's tip

Implementing a system of TQM has enormous implications for the management of the workforce. It is likely to result in recruitment and training and can have a positive effect on motivation. Do seek to explore these links when responding to high-mark examination questions in this area.

Quality standards

Revised

A **quality standard** is awarded to businesses that have put into place certain systems that enable certain quality targets to be met.

ISO 9000 is the standard most commonly available to businesses in the EU. The UK equivalent of this standard is BS 5750. Businesses have to meet criteria to receive certification that shows this standard is being met. They have to establish and maintain an effective quality system to demonstrate that products or services conform to it.

quality standard — awarded to businesses that have put into place certain systems that enable certain quality targets to be met

BSI and ISO systems are based on documentary evidence that specified procedures and processes are followed. Hence, they can become very bureaucratic.

Now test yourself

Tested

2 Draw up a table to show the advantages and disadvantages of implementing systems of (i) quality control and (ii) quality assurance. List the reasons why a business may opt to operate systems of quality assurance rather than a system of quality control.

Answers on p. 103

Effective operations: customer service

What is customer service?

Revised

Customer service is a range of activities designed to improve the degree of satisfaction experienced by a business's customers. One objective of customer service is to meet or exceed a customer's expectations from using the good or service.

Customer service can take a number of forms, including:

- **Personal assistance.** Offering customers advice and support while they are looking for a product or using a service is a common technique.

- **Online customer service.** Many firms offer customer service via the internet. For example, customers can purchase products 24 hours a day, 365 days every year. This approach allows customers to shop without leaving home or incurring travel costs.

> **customer service** — a range of activities designed to improve the degree of satisfaction experienced by a business's customers

Methods of meeting customer service expectations

Revised

There are a number of methods of meeting a customer's expectations:

- **Finding out what customers expect.** By understanding what a customer expects from a good or service, a business is able to ensure that it provides whatever is necessary to meet the customer's expectations. This is likely to involve the use of primary market research.

- **Recruiting the right employees and providing training.** This is important for all businesses, but arguably more so for those providing a service where there is greater contact between employees and customers. Employees should receive the necessary training to enable them to meet customers' expectations as fully as possible.

- **Communicating effectively.** Customers' expectations are more likely to be met by a business that communicates well with them. Examples include providing clear information on products or services and on prices and whom to ask for further information. Employees should have sufficient training to enable them to answer customers' questions efficiently.

- **Taking a long-term view of customer relationships.** Some customers may ask for special requirements, such as quick delivery, which may entail extra short-term expense. Meeting this requirement could offer great long-term benefits in the form of customer loyalty and positive publicity via word-of-mouth.

- **Implementing a quality system.** Quality control systems are designed to remove faulty products from the production system before they reach the customer. This approach to quality can be effective in helping to meet customer expectations, but it does assume that substandard products will be allowed to pass through the production system. Alternatively, a business might use a system of quality assurance, such as TQM, which aims to avoid any quality errors.

- **Quality standards.** Quality standards can be an important element of meeting customers' expectations. Standards such as ISO 9000 ensure that firms use systems designed to meet quality targets. Having these standards also shows that businesses have systems in place to rectify any failures to meet quality targets.

> **Examiner's tip**
>
> Think about how different businesses will meet their customers' expectations. This will help you to apply your knowledge on customer service. How might a family butcher meet customer expectations? Contrast this with the way in which a garden design company might do the same thing.

Figure 7.2 Key issues in customer service

Monitoring and improving customer service

Revised

Managers should not become complacent about their customer service provision. Businesses may find that rivals have improved their service by opening for longer hours or offering enhanced after-sales service. It is likely that consumer expectations will rise over time.

Businesses can monitor the levels of customer service using a range of techniques:

- asking customers to complete online surveys
- telephoning customers who have recently bought a product to enquire about their experiences
- leaving monitoring cards for customers to complete — this is common in hotels
- employing market research agencies to carry out monitoring work with a sample of customers

The techniques that a business deploys to monitor the quality of its customer service and the degree to which its customers' expectations are met will depend on the finance it has available to it.

> **Examiner's tip**
>
> A well-managed business will investigate weaknesses in its customer service provision before taking decisions on how to improve it. The actual approach taken will depend on the results of this research, the nature of the business and the market in which it trades.

The benefits of high levels of customer service

Revised

A business that offers high levels of customer service will receive a range of possible benefits:

- **The ability to charge premium prices.** Businesses that are recognised as meeting customers' expectations may be able to charge higher prices because demand is relatively price inelastic. This means customers are more likely to remain loyal to a business even when its prices rise.

- **The ability to use customer service as a USP.** A reputation for high-quality customer service can enable a business to differentiate its products from those sold by competitors. This can be used as a basis for promoting a product.

Exam practice answers and quick quizzes at **www.therevisionbutton.co.uk/myrevisionnotes**

- **The maintenance of customer loyalty.** Customers may be more likely to continue to purchase the goods or services of a particular business if they feel that their expectations are met. This can have positive effects on sales revenues and profits.

Effective operations: suppliers

Choosing effective suppliers

Revised

Suppliers provide businesses with products and services that are essential for the organisation to carry out its commercial activities. A supplier may provide:

- raw materials and fuel
- components such as electrical systems and tyres for car manufacturers
- services such as support on environmental protection or health and safety
- capital assets, such as buildings and machinery, which may be purchased infrequently

> **suppliers** — provide businesses with products and services that are essential for the organisation to carry out its commercial activities

A supplier will be considered effective if it meets a number of criteria:

- **Reliability and flexibility.** An effective supplier will always deliver on time and to the agreed specification. It will also be flexible and able to meet a sudden change in customer requirements — in terms of either volume or specification.

- **Ability to offer competitive prices.** An effective supplier meets the customer's expectations on price by operating efficiently itself. This helps customers to maintain profit margins and avoid adverse budget variances. An effective supplier will also control its own costs, especially during a period when inflation is rising.

- **Ability to meet the customer's specifications.** A manufacturer of organic foods will require organic ingredients. If a supplier is to be effective, it must be able to meet the precise needs of its customers. If it fails to do so, the business buying from the supplier may not be able to meet the expectations of its customers, thereby damaging its reputation and financial performance.

- **Payment terms.** Cash flow is an important factor for many businesses. If a supplier can offer trade credit (i.e. time to pay), this makes it very attractive as it delays cash outflows and can improve the customer's cash position. It is not unusual for suppliers to offer 30 or 60 days' trade credit in order to win customers.

A supplier is more likely to be judged effective if it has a long-term relationship with its customers. Many businesses seek to establish partnerships with suppliers. This happens when suppliers meet the conditions set out above, and in return the customers pay on the agreed date, offer fair prices and advise suppliers of any changes in their requirements well in advance.

> **Typical mistake**
>
> Do not fall into the trap of thinking that price is the most important factor in selecting a supplier. The key factor or factors will depend on the circumstances. For a small business it may be that the availability of favourable credit terms is a critical part of the decision.

Suppliers and a business's operational performance

An effective supplier offers a number of benefits to its businesses:

- **Enabling the customer business to operate within agreed budgets**. If suppliers deliver products at the agreed price, businesses should not suffer an adverse variance on budgets.
- **Assisting the customer business in meeting the expectations of its own customers.** It does this by always delivering the required quantity on time and to the agreed specification.
- **Offering support and advice on the supplies it provides.** For example, a business supplying technical component might provide advice on relevant technological developments.
- **Responding quickly to changes in the size of its orders.** This enables the customer business to meet seasonal demand or unexpected orders.
- **Helping the business to operate its quality systems and meet its targets.** This can be done by providing a reliable service and meeting orders promptly and precisely.

> **Now test yourself**
>
> 3   Design a diagram to summarise the ways in which using an effective supplier may help a business to improve its financial performance (cash flow and profits).
>
> **Answers on p. 103**
>
> Tested

Using technology in operations

Types of technology used in operations

Technology is changing quickly and affects how businesses produce goods and services as well as the products themselves. Technological developments that may affect production include:

- more advanced computer systems, allowing, for example, automated stock control systems and electronic data interchange
- the internet, which enhances a business's ability to promote and sell products and its ability to communicate with customers
- computer-aided manufacture (CAM), where manufacturers use robots as an integral part of the production process
- computer-aided design (CAD), which can be linked to CAM systems

Changes in technology mean that even small businesses can benefit from developments in stock control and design technology. This assists them to improve the quality of their product or service, and to compete with larger-scale competitors.

The development of CAD has made new products easier to design, store and alter. Modern software can also be used to estimate the cost of newly designed products. Technology has revolutionised manufacturing too. Computer-aided manufacturing is used by manufacturing firms of all sizes. Computers control the machines on the production line, saving labour and costs, and CAM systems can be linked to CAD technology to transform the entire process.

Issues in introducing and updating technology   Revised

Benefits of new and updated technology

New technology offers businesses and consumers a range of benefits:

- It reduces unit costs of production, enhancing the competitiveness of the business concerned. For example, it allows small publishers to send books electronically to be printed overseas, where costs are lower.

- For high-technology products, such as games consoles, it offers the opportunity to charge a premium price until the competition catches up. Such price skimming is likely to boost profits.

- Technology offers the chance to improve quality by, for example, ensuring a consistent standard of quality through the use of CAM.

- Small to medium-sized businesses may benefit from technology through improved productivity. Using technology efficiently may enable employees to work more efficiently. For example, EPOS (electronic point of sale) systems record information on sales and prices, and can be operated by the checkout operator in a shop as a routine part of work. EPOS adjusts stock levels and re-orders stock automatically as well as providing data to calculate sales revenue figures.

- It may allow access to new markets: for example, the internet allows potteries to sell worldwide.

- The use of technology can reduce waste. Modern water control systems in commercial buildings recycle rainwater and other water for re-use within the business.

Costs of new and updated technology

New technology also poses difficulties for many businesses:

- It can be a drain on an organisation's capital. Firms may experience difficulty in raising the funds required to install high-technology equipment or to research a new product.

- It almost inevitably requires training of the existing workforce and perhaps recruitment of new employees. Both actions can create considerable costs for businesses.

- Its introduction may be met with opposition from existing employees, especially if job security is threatened. This may lead to industrial relations problems.

Now test yourself   Tested

4   Technology is a topic with links to many other areas of the specification. Divide a sheet of paper into four sections and label these as (i) marketing, (ii) finance, (iii) operations management and (iv) people in business. In each of the four sections compile a list of the implications for that function of the business of a decision to use new technology in producing a product or in the product itself.

Answers on p. 103

Check your understanding

1 State the formula used to calculate unit costs.

2 Define the terms 'quality' and 'customer service'.

3 Distinguish between quality control and quality assurance.

4 Define the term 'supplier'.

5 State the formula used to calculate capacity utilisation. How should answers to this calculation be expressed?

6 What is the difference between computer-aided design (CAD) and computer-aided manufacturing (CAM) systems?

7 What is a quality standard?

8 Describe two ways in which a business might monitor the quality of its customer service.

9 Briefly explain one way in which a business might remove spare capacity from within the business.

10 What is a 'non-standard' order? Why might it pose a problem for a business?

11 Explain a possible benefit to a business of implementing a system of quality assurance such as TQM.

12 Why might a business benefit from taking a long-term view of its relationships with its customers?

13 Explain how employees might benefit and be disadvantaged by the introduction of more technology into a business's production processes.

14 Explain two ways in which an airline (such as KLM) might increase its capacity.

15 Explain two difficulties that a business may face when updating its production line technology.

Answers on p. 104

Exam practice

Ruffett Technology Ltd manufactures equipment that is used in hospitals, such as electronically operated beds and machinery used during surgery. The company has enjoyed steadily rising sales in recent years and profits have doubled since 2006, though its cash position is weaker. Its sales of hospital beds have been buoyant. The company sold 18,000 beds in 2010, giving its bed manufacturing factory a capacity utilisation figure of 90%. Its sales in 2011 rose by 1,500 and the factory's capacity was unchanged.

However, there has been a small increase in the number of complaints about the company's products (1.94% of sales were returned) and the management team is concerned. A decision has been taken to implement a system of total quality management (TQM). The company's highly skilled employees have not been consulted about this change.

A second change is to be introduced alongside TQM. The management team believe that increasing the use of technology on the production line would benefit the company. The intention is to use CAD and CAM systems and to have the new technology operational 'as soon as possible'.

Questions

a Calculate the level of capacity utilisation in the bed manufacturing factory in 2011. [6]

b Analyse the benefits the company may receive from implementing a system of TQM next year. [9]

c Do you agree with the management team's decision to increase the use of technology on its production line? [15]

Answers and quick quiz 7 online

Online

8 Marketing and the competitive environment

Effective marketing

The nature and purpose of marketing
Revised

What is marketing and what is its purpose in business?

Marketing is the management process that identifies, anticipates and supplies customer requirements efficiently and profitably.

Some argue that the purpose of marketing is to be the guiding philosophy for all the activities of a business. According to Peter Drucker, 'there is only one valid definition of business purpose: to create a customer'.

> **marketing** — the management process that identifies, anticipates and supplies customer requirements efficiently and profitably

The distinction between consumer marketing and business-to-business marketing

Consumer marketing encompasses those activities involved in selling a product to an individual who is the end user: that is, the person who consumes the product. This is also described as business-to-consumer marketing or B2C marketing.

In contrast, business-to-business marketing (B2B marketing) describes the range of activities undertaken by one business when marketing its products to another business.

Benefits and drawbacks of niche and mass marketing
Revised

Niche marketing occurs when businesses identify and satisfy the demands of small segments of a larger market. A well-known example of businesses engaging in niche marketing is the radio station Classic FM. Classic FM serves the niche of people who wish to listen to popular classical music.

> **niche marketing** — when businesses identify and satisfy the demands of small segments of a larger market

The advantages and disadvantages of niche marketing are:

- The first company to identify a niche market can often gain a dominant market position as consumers become loyal to the product — even if its price is higher.
- Niche markets can be highly profitable, as companies operating in them often have the opportunity to charge premium prices.
- Because sales may be relatively low, firms operating in niche markets may not be able to spread fixed overheads over sufficient sales to attain acceptable profit margins.

- If a niche market proves to be profitable, it is likely to attract new competition, making it less attractive to the companies that first discovered the market.

Mass marketing occurs when businesses aim their products at most of the available market. Many small and medium-sized businesses sell in mass markets.

Businesses must be able to produce on a large scale if they are to sell successfully in a mass market. This may mean that the firm has to invest heavily in resources such as buildings, machinery and vehicles. Often firms have to be price competitive to flourish in mass markets, or to have a USP that makes the company and its products distinctive.

> **mass marketing** — when businesses aim their products at most of the available market

> **Examiner's tip**
>
> This is a common topic for examination questions. Examiners frequently ask whether a move into a niche market, or from a niche to a mass market, is a good strategy. You should consider the type of market and the type of firm in developing your answer, and make sure you apply your response to the scenario throughout.

What is the marketing mix?

Revised ☐

The **marketing mix** refers to the main variables comprising a firm's marketing strategy. The four main elements of the mix are:

- **product** — including design, features and functions
- **price** — pricing strategies and tactics
- **promotion** — a range of activities including advertising, public relations (PR) and branding
- **place** — distribution channels and retail outlets

These elements are sometimes referred to as the **four Ps**. Some writers identify more than four Ps, including factors such as **packaging** and **people**.

> **marketing mix** — the main variables comprising a firm's marketing strategy

> **Typical mistake**
>
> When responding to questions about the marketing mix do not write about all four elements, as you are unlikely to have time to develop all points fully. Choose the most important two elements and write about those.

Using the marketing mix: product

Influences on development of new goods and services

Revised ☐

A number of factors have an effect upon the development of new goods and services:

- **Technology.** Developments in technology are at the heart of many of the new products that come on to the market. For example, advances in battery technology have helped to generate a range of more efficient electric cars. Firms use these technological advances as the basis for the development of new products that meet the needs of consumers more fully.

- **Competitors' actions.** A competitor producing a new product can be a spur to a rival to produce something that is at least as good, if not better. Hotels have improved their services by, for example, offering guests a choice of different types of pillow to enhance comfort.

- **The entrepreneurial skills of managers and owners.** One of the talents of successful entrepreneurs is creativity. The skill of being able to think up new ideas for goods and services that fit with customer needs leads to the development of many new products.

The importance of unique selling points

Revised

Businesses commonly add value by creating a **unique selling point or proposition (USP)** for their products. A USP allows a business to differentiate its products from others in the market. This can help the business in a number of ways:

- The business can base its advertising campaigns around the (real or perceived) difference between its product and those of its rivals.
- Having a USP assists in encouraging brand loyalty, as its gives customers a reason to continue to buy that particular business's product.
- A USP commonly allows the firm to charge a premium price for the product.

USP — allows a business to differentiate its products from others in the market

Product portfolio analysis

Revised

The product life cycle

The **product life cycle** is the theory that all products follow a similar pattern throughout their life. Products take varying amounts of time to pass through these stages. The Mars bar was launched in the 1920s and is still going strong. In contrast, modern motor cars are expected to have a life cycle of about 10 years. The stages are outlined below and illustrated in Figure 8.1.

1 **Development.** Firms undertake research and development to create new products that will be their future best sellers. Many products fall by the wayside, as they do not meet the demands of consumers. This can be a very expensive stage and cash flow is expected to be negative.

2 **Introduction.** This stage commences with the product's initial appearance on the market. At this time, sales are zero and the product

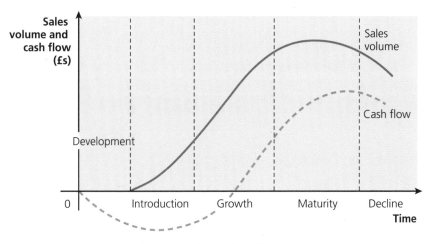

Figure 8.1 The product life cycle

has a negative cash flow. Sales should begin to rise, providing the company with some revenue. However, costs will remain high. The failure rate for new products is high — 60% to 90%. Promotion can be expensive and cash flow will remain negative. The price may have to be high to recoup the high initial launch costs.

3 **Growth.** During the growth stage, sales rise rapidly and a firm's cash flow can improve considerably. The business's profits per unit sold are likely to be at a maximum. This is because firms tend to charge a high price at this stage, particularly if the product is innovatory. Firms with a technically superior good may well engage in price skimming (see p. 88). The growth stage is critical to a product's survival. The product's success will depend on how competitors react to it.

4 **Maturity.** During the maturity stage, the sales curve peaks and begins to decline. Both cash flow and profits also decline. This stage is characterised by intense competition with other brands. Competitors emphasise improvements and differences in their versions of the product. At this stage, consumers of the product know a lot about it and require specialist deals to attract their interest.

5 **Decline.** During the decline stage, sales fall rapidly. New technology or a new product change may cause product sales to decline sharply. When this happens, marketing managers consider eliminating unprofitable products. At this stage, promotional efforts will be cut too.

Extension strategies

Firms may attempt to prolong the life of a product as it enters the decline stage by implementing extension strategies. They may use techniques such as the following:

- **Finding new markets for existing products.** Some companies selling baby milk have targeted less economically developed countries.
- **Changing the appearance or packaging.** Some motor manufacturers have produced old models of cars with new colours or other features to extend the lives of their products.

The product mix

A well-organised business will plan its product range so that it has products in each of the major stages of the life cycle: as one product reaches decline, replacements are entering the growth and maturity stages of their lives (see Figure 8.2). This means that there will be a constant flow

Examiner's tip

For all major theories, such as the product life cycle, you should be able to give some assessment of the theory's strengths and weaknesses. This will help you to write evaluatively as well as confirming your understanding.

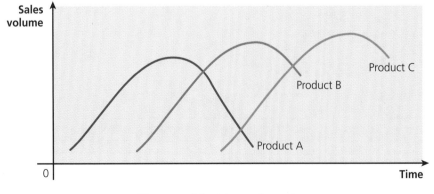

Figure 8.2 A healthy product mix

of income from products in the mature phase of their lives to finance the development of new products.

The Boston matrix

The Boston matrix was developed by the Boston Consulting Group. The matrix allows businesses to undertake product portfolio analysis based on the product's market growth rate and its market share.

The matrix, as shown in Figures 8.3 and 8.4, places products into four categories:

- **Star products** have a dominant share of the market and good prospects for growth.
- **Cash cows** are products with a dominant share of the market but low prospects for growth.
- **Dogs** have a low share of the market and no prospects for growth.
- **Problem children** are products that have a small share of a growing market.

A number of conclusions can be drawn from the Boston matrix:

- Firms should avoid having too many products in any single category. Obviously, firms do not want lots of dogs, but they also need to avoid having too many stars and problem children.
- Products in the top half of the chart are in the early stages of their life cycle and are in growing markets, but the cost of developing and promoting them will not have been recovered.

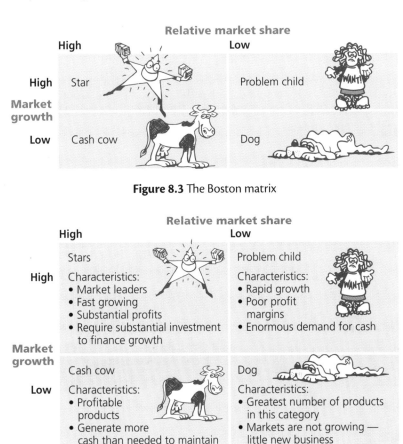

Figure 8.3 The Boston matrix

Relative market share

	High	Low
High	Stars Characteristics: • Market leaders • Fast growing • Substantial profits • Require substantial investment to finance growth	Problem child Characteristics: • Rapid growth • Poor profit margins • Enormous demand for cash
Low	Cash cow Characteristics: • Profitable products • Generate more cash than needed to maintain market share	Dog Characteristics: • Greatest number of products in this category • Markets are not growing — little new business • Operate at a cost disadvantage

Market growth

Figure 8.4 Features of the components of the marketing mix

● Continuing production of cash cows will provide the necessary cash to develop the newer products.
● Firms need problem child products as they may become tomorrow's cash cows.

Now test yourself

1 Construct a table to set out the advantages and disadvantages to a business of moving from a niche market into a mass market.
2 Write notes to explain the difference between the Boston matrix and the product life cycle and how managers may use them to make decisions about the portfolio of products to be sold.

Answers on p. 104

Using the marketing mix: promotion

What is promotion?

Promotion is bringing consumers' attention to a product or business. Promotion aims to achieve targets including:

● to attract new customers and retain existing customers
● to improve the position of the business in the market
● to ensure the survival and growth of the business
● to increase awareness of a product

promotion — bringing consumers' attention to a product or business

Examiner's tip

It is easy to think that promotion just means advertising. Figure 8.5 emphasises that this is not the case. Good quality answers to examination questions on this topic will demonstrate awareness of the circumstances in which each of the elements of the promotional mix might be appropriate.

The elements of the promotional mix

The **promotional mix** is the combination of methods used by businesses to communicate with prospective customers to inform them of their products and to persuade them to buy these products.

promotional mix — the combination of methods used by businesses to communicate with prospective customers to inform them of their products and to persuade them to buy these products

Figure 8.5 The promotional mix

Advertising

Advertising is a paid form of non-personal communication using mass media to change the attitudes and buying behaviour of consumers. Advertising can be separated into two types:

- **Informative advertising.** This is designed to increase consumer awareness of a product by providing consumers with factual information. Such adverts centre on the prices and features of the products being advertised.
- **Persuasive advertising.** This attempts to get consumers to purchase a particular product by, for example, claiming that the product is better than the competition.

Sales promotions and merchandising

Merchandising is in-store promotional activity by manufacturers or retailers at the point of sale. Merchandising can be important when consumers make purchasing decisions at the point of sale and a variety of rival products are on display in stores — confectionery is an example.

Other forms of sales promotion include:

- special offers and competitions
- in-store demonstrations
- coupons, vouchers and free gifts

These forms of promotion may be used when rival businesses wish to avoid starting a price war, which they might not win. Merchandising can be relatively cheap, but is not good at targeting specific groups of consumers.

Packaging

Packaging emphasises the attractiveness of the product and informs consumers of its features, functions and contents. Packaging also protects the good during its distribution to ensure that it reaches the consumer in perfect condition.

Exhibitions and trade fairs

These are events staged to attract all those people involved in a particular market, both sellers and buyers. An example is the Motor Show held in Birmingham each year.

Branding

This establishes an identity for a product that distinguishes it from the competition. Successful branding allows higher prices to be charged and can extend the product's life cycle by creating customer loyalty. Brand loyalty occurs when consumers regularly purchase particular products and it can allow firms to charge higher prices.

Personal selling

Personal selling involves visits by a firm's sales representatives to prospective customers. This may be used more in business-to-business selling, or in selling expensive products such as double glazing. Personal selling is a relatively expensive method of raising public awareness of a product.

> **advertising** — a paid form of non-personal communication using mass media to change the attitudes and buying behaviour of consumers

Public relations

PR is promoting the company's image to establish a favourable public attitude towards the company. Public relations aims to improve the image of a business and its products in the expectation of increasing sales through sponsoring sporting or cultural activities or making donations to worthwhile causes.

Influences on the choice of promotional mix   Revised ☐

Managers will take into account a range of factors when deciding on the precise promotional mix to be deployed:

- **The product's position in its life cycle.** A newly launched product is likely to need heavy advertising to inform customers of its existence and the benefits it provides. An established product may use sales promotions to persuade customers to buy it.

- **The type of product.** Expensive products and those where design is a major element will make greater use of exhibitions and trade fairs in the promotional mix. This element of the mix is important, for example, to firms selling homes and fashion products.

- **The finance available to the business.** Firms with larger budgets may engage more in public relations and personal selling, as these methods of promotion are expensive.

- **Where consumers make purchasing decisions.** For businesses that sell products that are purchased on impulse, often at the point of sale, merchandising and packaging may be particularly important. The attractiveness of the wrappers and the positioning of the product within shops may be vital.

- **Competitors' actions.** If a business's rivals are engaging in heavy advertising or extensive sales promotions, it is likely that the business will respond similarly. This is more likely if the business trades in a market where there is relatively little product differentiation.

> **Typical mistake**
>
> Many students respond to questions about the promotional mix by writing about the marketing mix. Do not confuse these two concepts.

Using the marketing mix: pricing

The pricing strategies used by businesses   Revised ☐

The **price of a product** is simply the amount that a business expects a customer to pay to purchase the good or service.

Pricing strategies are the medium- to long-term pricing plans that a business adopts. There are four principal pricing strategies:

- **Price skimming.** Price skimming is often used when a new, innovative product is launched. It is unlikely that this product will face direct competition immediately. By setting a high price, the business will achieve limited sales but with a high profit margin on each. This allows the firm to recoup some of the product's development costs. The price is lowered when competitors enter the market.

> **price of a product** — the amount that a business expects a customer to pay to purchase the good or service
>
> **pricing strategies** — the medium- to long-term pricing plans that a business adopts

- **Price leadership.** Price leadership is used for established products with strong brand images. The firm adopting this strategy will probably dominate the market and other businesses will usually follow its lead.
- **Penetration pricing.** Firms entering a market with products similar to those already available may use penetration pricing. The price is set deliberately low to gain a foothold in the market. The expectation is that, once the product is established, the price will be increased to boost profit margins.
- **Price taking.** Price takers set their prices equal to the 'going rate' or the established market price. This is a common pricing strategy for small and medium-sized businesses. Price takers have no influence over the market price, as they are normally one of many smallish firms competing for business.

Once a business has determined its pricing strategy, it may employ a number of pricing tactics. Pricing tactics are a series of pricing techniques that are normally used only over the short term to achieve specific goals. They include:

- **Loss leaders.** This entails setting prices very low (often below the cost of production) to attract customers. Businesses using this tactic hope that customers will purchase other (full-price) products while purchasing the loss leader.
- **Special-offer pricing.** This approach involves reduced prices for a limited period of time or offers such as 'three for the price of two'.

> **Typical mistake**
>
> Some students write about pricing tactics when the question asks about pricing strategies. If a question asks about strategies, you must write about relevant pricing actions that a business can take in the long term, and not short-term tactical decisions.

Influences on pricing decisions
Revised

There is a range of factors that might influence a firm in its pricing decisions. A firm is more likely to select strategies and tactics that result in low prices if it is seeking to expand its market share. This type of approach may also be more popular with businesses that are in a financially strong position. In contrast, a business that is selling a product which is highly differentiated or facing increasing popularity may opt for higher price levels.

Price elasticity of demand

One key factor influencing managers in their pricing decisions is price elasticity of demand. **Price elasticity of demand** measures the extent to which the level of demand for a product is sensitive to price changes. An increase in price is almost certain to reduce demand, while a price reduction can be expected to increase the level of demand. However, the extent to which demand changes following a given price change is less predictable.

> **price elasticity of demand** — the extent to which the level of demand for a product is sensitive to price changes

Demand is said to be price elastic if it is sensitive to price changes. So, an increase in price will result in a significant lowering of demand and a fall in the firm's revenue. Products with a lot of competition are price elastic, as an increase in price will result in substantial loss of sales.

Price inelastic demand exists when price changes have relatively little effect on the level of demand. Examples of products with price inelastic demand are petrol and other essentials. Price elasticity of demand (PED) is calculated by the formula:

$$PED = \frac{\text{percentage change in quantity demanded}}{\text{percentage change in price}}$$

For example, if a price rise of 5% leads to a fall in demand of 10%, PED = −10/+5 = −2.

The answers to PED calculations are always negative because there is always a negative figure in the calculation. If price rises, demand falls; and if price falls, demand rises.

If demand for a product is price inelastic, a price change will result in a smaller percentage change in quantity demanded. As a result, the coefficient of elasticity for a product in inelastic demand will be between 0 and −1. So products with elasticity coefficients of −0.25 or −0.6 will have inelastic demand.

In contrast, a product with price-elastic demand will have a coefficient of elasticity somewhere between −1 and −∞. So a product with a value of −2 will have elastic demand.

The important thing about PED is that it determines how a price change will affect the business's sales or total revenue.

Firms calculate their sales revenue by multiplying the sales volume by the price at which they sell their products. Elasticity plays an important part in this calculation. For example, a firm facing price inelastic demand would enjoy higher sales revenue if it raised its price. This is because the increase in price would have relatively little impact on the volume of sales. However, in the case of price-elastic demand, a price cut would be likely to lead to increased revenue (see Table 8.1).

> **Examiner's tip**
>
> You will not be asked to calculate PED directly in an examination. You should understand the business implications of price elastic and inelastic demand, such as the effect of a given price change on the business's total revenue.

Table 8.1 Price, elasticity and total revenue

	Price rise	Price cut
Elastic demand	Total revenue falls	Total revenue rises
Inelastic demand	Total revenue rises	Total revenue falls

Firms would prefer to sell products with demand that is price inelastic, as this gives greater freedom in selecting a pricing strategy and more opportunity to raise prices, total revenue and profits.

Businesses can adopt a number of techniques to make demand for their products more price inelastic:

- **Differentiating products from those of competitors.** Making a product significantly different from those of competitors can increase brand loyalty. Consumers are more likely to continue to purchase a product when its price rises if it has unique characteristics.
- **Reducing competition through takeovers and mergers.** In recent years, many markets have seen fewer, but larger firms competing with each other. This process results in fewer products being available to the consumer and may mean that demand will be less responsive to price.

> **Now test yourself**
>
> 3 Design a diagram to show the pricing strategies available to businesses and the major influences on pricing decisions.
>
> Answers on p. 104
>
> Tested ☐

Using the marketing mix: place

The **distribution of a product** refers to the range of activities necessary to make the product available to customers.

> **distribution of a product** — the range of activities necessary to make the product available to customers

Choosing appropriate outlets and distributors

Revised

The choice of an outlet or a distributor to supply the products to outlets must fit with the rest of the product's marketing mix. For example, it is vital that if the product is to be sold cheaply, possibly to increase market share, then suitable outlets are chosen. In this situation, a cost-cutting retail outlet might be appropriate, so that the benefit of low prices is passed on to the final customer.

Other factors that a business might take into account when choosing outlets and distributors include:

- **Location.** Businesses will seek outlets and distributors in areas where their target customers live and where few competitors operate.
- **Credit terms.** A newly established or struggling enterprise might opt for outlets or distributors that do not request long periods of trade credit. This can help to protect a business's cash flow.
- **Willingness to display products in prominent positions.** For some products (e.g. foods and confectionery), a good position in a retail outlet is an essential part of successful distribution.

Types of distribution channel

Revised

There are a number of different forms of distribution. The three main channels are illustrated in Figure 8.6.

- **Traditional.** Many small retailers buy stock from wholesalers, as they do not purchase sufficient quantities to buy directly from producers. Wholesalers offer other benefits besides small quantities, such as advice, credit and delivery, although they can be expensive.
- **Modern.** Major retailers such as Marks and Spencer purchase directly from manufacturers and arrange their own distribution. They

Figure 8.6 The channels of distribution

can do this because they buy huge quantities of products and are able to negotiate large discounts that more than cover the costs of distribution. As a consequence, they can offer discounts to consumers, enhancing their market position.

- **Direct.** This is a rapidly growing channel of distribution. It is attractive to many firms because it lowers the prices at which they can sell products to the consumer. Many small businesses have started to sell their products directly to customers using the internet.

The choice of a distribution channel will be influenced by a number of factors:

- **The type of product.** Products that are difficult to transport because of their bulk, fragility or perishable nature are more likely to be distributed direct to avoid incurring additional costs. Producers selling large amounts of relatively low-priced products are more likely to use a wholesaler as it is expensive to store this type of product.

- **The nature of the market.** Businesses selling in dispersed markets usually require the services of wholesalers as they have the resources to supply in these circumstances.

- **The technical complexity of the product.** Technically complex products (such as laptops) are better distributed when the customer and the producer can easily contact each other to solve problems of installation or operation.

> **Typical mistake**
>
> Don't ignore place or distribution. It is sometimes called 'the forgotten P' and students often respond poorly to questions that are set on it. You should know the different distribution methods and which are appropriate in different circumstances.

Designing an effective marketing mix

The influences on the marketing mix · Revised

Managers take a range of factors into account when designing the marketing mix for a product (see Figure 8.7).

Finance

The level of profits that a business earns can impact on the price that it charges. A profitable business is able to cut prices significantly, at least in

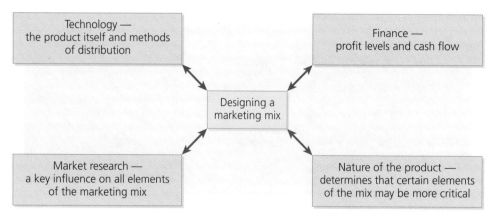

Figure 8.7 Influences on the marketing mix

the short term. Its financial reserves also enable it to engage in extensive promotional campaigns, including PR activities.

Another aspect of finance that affects the marketing mix is that a business with a healthy cash flow will be able to extend the range of outlets it uses by offering favourable trade credit terms.

The nature of the product

The type of product can influence which elements of the mix are emphasised. An insurance firm may spend heavily on advertising to generate large numbers of enquiries to win an acceptable number of customers. In contrast, a portrait painter may rely on the quality of the product and word-of-mouth promotion to achieve sales.

Technology

Some products that possess the latest technology may use advertising to inform potential customers of their existence and benefits. They will have high prices to maximise short-term profits and cover the costs of research and development. Technology has also affected the place element of the marketing mix. Developments have allowed publishers of music and books to distribute their products using internet downloads.

Market research

Primary market research may be the most importance influence in designing a marketing mix. Its findings may provide information to help to make judgements on the form, functions and design of the product. The research may uncover information on prices that consumers will be willing to pay and the type of purchasers. Market research may also determine pricing strategies.

The importance of an integrated marketing mix
Revised

An integrated marketing mix is one that fits together. If a business is selling a premium product, the entire mix should support this. The elements might be constructed as follows:

- **Product.** This should be high quality in terms of design, innovativeness, features or functions.
- **Price.** The price is likely to be high (skimming) to reflect the premium nature of the product.
- **Place.** The business would seek outlets that reflect the quality or exclusivity of the product.
- **Promotion.** This would be targeted at the people who are likely to purchase the product.

If the marketing mix is inconsistent, consumers may be deterred from purchasing the product, thereby depressing sales and profits. In the case of a premium product, a low price might be a mistake as it may lead some consumers to think the product is not premium quality.

> **Examiner's tip**
>
> Remember that marketing mixes can be integrated in different ways depending on factors such as price and the target audience. For example, easyJet and Rolls-Royce have markedly different marketing mixes, but both are integrated.

Marketing and competitiveness

Market structure

There are a number of ways of judging a market. We can consider its size or growth rate or the structure of the market and how it influences the marketing behaviour of a business. The structure of a market takes into account two factors:

- **The number of businesses in the market.** If a business faces a greater number of competitors, it is likely to encounter tough competition. This statement is more likely to be true if the business faces a lot of nearby competitors that sell products which are similar, and if they are able to sell their products at similar or lower prices. Businesses in a competitive market might spend heavily on promotion and focus on providing top-quality service.
- **The relative size and power of the businesses.** It is not uncommon for small and medium-sized business to compete with much larger rivals. In such circumstances, smaller enterprises may be unable to compete in terms of price or advertising. In this case the product itself and the associated quality of service may be highly important factors.

Barriers to entry

The structure of the market can influence the marketing actions taken by a business in other ways. An established business with a degree of market power (in terms of profits or market share) may take actions to prevent new rivals entering the market. Such actions are designed to establish barriers to entry and prevent or restrict free entry by firms to a given market. Barriers include:

- **Establishing and extending brand loyalty.** This can be encouraged by offering discounts to regular customers or by giving customers long-term benefits through loyalty card schemes.
- **Seeking legal restrictions.** Many businesses may seek to obtain patents on products or processes that they produce, thus preventing other businesses from supplying similar products.

It is logical for businesses to seek to erect and maintain barriers to protect market share. They may do this by introducing new brands to dilute the effect of a new supplier entering the market or spend heavily on marketing to increase the entry costs of potential market entrants.

Competitiveness is the extent to which a firm is successful in outperforming its rivals in the marketplace. Competitiveness can take a number of forms.

> **competitiveness** — the extent to which a firm is successful in outperforming its rivals in the marketplace

Price competitiveness

A price-competitive firm is able to provide a product to its customers at a lower price than its rivals. However, this alone is not sufficient to provide a competitive advantage. The benefits provided by the product must also at least equal those of its rivals.

Product competitiveness

This form of competitiveness is based on the benefits provided by a product. If a business provides a top-quality product or enhanced levels of customer service, the consumer will receive greater benefits and may prefer the product to those supplied by its rivals. In these circumstances, customers will be willing to pay higher prices for the product.

Competitiveness through image

Some businesses spend heavily on promotion to build up an image for the business or product that is attractive to its target audience. Some businesses have developed an environmentally friendly image as a means of creating a strong competitive position.

Developing a unique selling point

By having a particular feature or function that differentiates its products from those of other companies, the business may be able to win customers from its rivals. This form of competitiveness is especially valuable if the USP can be protected by a patent or copyright.

A firm that has a competitive advantage will need to take action to maintain this advantage in the longer term. Changes in technology or in consumers' tastes can erode a competitive advantage.

Examiner's tip

The determinants of competitiveness vary according to the circumstances of a business and the market in which it trades. The case study on a Unit 2 examination paper will offer vital information on this if there is a question on competitiveness.

Methods of improving competitiveness
Revised

A business can improve its competitiveness by working on any of the forms of competitiveness outlined in the previous section.

Improving price competitiveness

This relies on reducing the costs of production:

- increasing the productivity of the workforce to reduce the labour cost of producing the product
- using less of more expensive resources and more of cheaper resources in production
- using cheaper sources of supplies of raw materials without compromising quality
- reducing the number of substandard products to reduce 'wasted' expenditure

Improving product competitiveness

Businesses often advertise 'new, improved' products. The business may have reduced the size of a product such as a laptop or increased the quality of its customer service. The nature of product competitiveness will vary according to the product. For example, a public house might open for longer hours, while a house builder may improve the specifications of its properties.

Improving image competitiveness

A business can create a more positive image by:

- being seen to protect the environment through operating recycling schemes, using sustainable resources and disposing of its waste products responsibly
- treating its employees fairly and with respect, offering ongoing training and opportunities for personal development
- contributing to community schemes such as clearing up litter and financing youth clubs

Developing a unique selling point

Anything that differentiates a business and its products from the others in the market can form the basis of competitive advantage. The quality of customer service may be important to businesses that are supplying services. This could be achieved by investing regularly in staff training or operating an effective recruitment system to employ the best-quality employees possible.

Examiner's tip

Competitiveness is an integrating topic and you can draw on any element of the AS specification to support your arguments and not just marketing. For example, improving capacity utilisation will help a business to become more competitive.

Now test yourself

Tested

4 Divide a sheet of paper into four sections and label them as (i) marketing, (ii) finance, (iii) operations management and (iv) people in business. For each section identify and explain three ways in which relevant techniques could be used to improve a business's competitiveness.

Answers on p. 104

Check your understanding

Tested

1 Define the term 'marketing'.
2 Distinguish between niche and mass marketing.
3 State four elements of the promotional mix.
4 State the four elements of the marketing mix.
5 Define the term 'competitiveness'.
6 State two barriers to entry that a business may face when entering a market.
7 List three factors that may determine a business's competitiveness.
8 Explain the difference between price elastic and price inelastic demand.
9 Using examples, explain the difference between a pricing tactic and a pricing strategy.
10 Outline the circumstances in which a business might decide to use a strategy of price skimming.
11 Explain the difference between a cash cow and a problem child as elements of the Boston matrix.
12 Outline two ways in which a business might improve its image competitiveness.
13 Explain two ways in which a business might make demand for its products more price inelastic.
14 Explain two influences on the promotional mix of a newly opened restaurant.
15 Explain the consequences for a brewery of having too many of its products in the maturity stage of the product life cycle at the same time.

Answers on p. 105

Exam practice

Prestige Hotels operates a chain of hotels located in historic English towns and cities such as Oxford, Shrewsbury and Chester. It operates in a niche market selling an expensive product to tourists, mainly from America. The company has suffered slowly declining profits in recent years and has struggled to compete in terms of quality of product with its rivals, and its management team is keen to increase brand loyalty. Its prices are about 5% below those of its closest rivals currently, though high compared with mainstream hotels.

The company's managers want to improve the competitiveness of the business to improve its long-term profitability. They have conducted some primary market research which has revealed that price elasticity of demand for its products is −0.3. The research has shown that the level of demand in the niche market has fallen at an increasing rate and by 20% over the last three years. One encouraging trend, however, is rising sales to tourists from China.

Questions

a Explain two benefits to the company of developing increased brand loyalty. [6]

b Analyse the benefits the company may receive from remaining in the niche market. [9]

c The best way for the company to improve its competitiveness is to reduce its prices. Do you agree? Justify your view. [15]

Answers and quick quiz 8 online

Online

Answers

Chapter 1

Now test yourself

1 Any four of the following:
- A clear idea or vision.
- Creativity (the ability to develop new ideas).
- The ability to turn good ideas into saleable products.
- Commitment to the idea and business.
- Willing to take risks.
- The ability to learn from mistakes and build on successes.

2 Any three of the following:
- The business may suffer from a shortage of cash (too few inflows and too many outflows).
- Insufficient customers leading to inadequate revenue and losses.
- Competitors introduce new products, cut prices or advertise more, resulting in a lack of customers.
- The entrepreneur may lack some essential skills such as the ability to manage people or finance.

3 Three examples include:
- The loss of salary that would have been earned in the well-paid job.
- The loss of the possibility of future promotions in the job.
- The loss of status that may have accompanied the well-paid job.

4 The major reasons include:
- The satisfaction that arises from creating a successful business.
- An entrepreneur wishes to develop an idea into a commercially successful product.
- The chance to be 'your own boss' and not to have to take orders from anyone.

5

Government support includes
• Education and training at school and for adults.
• Business loan guarantees.
• Business Link — a website providing a range of information.

Other support includes
• Venture capitalists provide advice and support (as well as finance).
• Banks offer a range of support for entrepreneurs.

6 (i) Brainstorming generates a high volume of ideas relatively cheaply, a small number of which may be of value.

(ii) Inventions can produce unique products that meet a demand and are not supplied by other businesses. An example is the wind-up radio invented by Trevor Baylis.

(iii) Market research enables an entrepreneur to discover the needs of potential customers and to design and supply products that meet these needs precisely.

7 Buying a franchise as a means of starting a new business:

Advantages
• Risk is reduced by using a successful and tested business idea.
• The entrepreneur can receive advice on matters of business management.
• The new enterprise may benefit from the franchisor's advertising campaigns.

Disadvantages
• The entrepreneur has less control over the business and can make fewer decisions.
• The initial costs of purchasing a franchise can be high, especially if it is well known such as McDonald's.
• The franchisee will have to pay a percentage of revenue, thereby reducing profit margins.

8 Resources include the services of all types of labour, land and other natural resources, capital including money, and materials and components.

The transformation process converts inputs into outputs.

This process may involve changing the nature of substances, supplying information that is available elsewhere, or retrieving resources and transporting them.

9 In your mind map, the key pieces of information should include aims and objectives, the products to be produced, sources of finance, market research plan, budgets and cash-flow forecasts and resources to be used.

Sources may include Business Link, venture capitalists, banks, small business advisers.

10 My choices are as follows (yours may be different):
- entrepreneur
- risk
- opportunity cost
- adding value
- business plan

Check your understanding

1 An entrepreneur is a person who is willing to take a risk in starting a new enterprise.

2 Risk is the possibility of incurring some misfortune or loss. Rewards are those things that an entrepreneur receives in return for taking the risk of starting a new business. The most obvious reward is money.

3 Opportunity cost is the next best alternative forgone. The opportunity cost of starting a business might be the salary that is given up. The opportunity cost of purchasing a new delivery vehicle might be a training course for some members of staff.

4 A creative person is likely to have a number of ideas for a business product and may be able to spot gaps in a market. A creative person may also be able to design effective marketing campaigns to persuade potential customers to buy the new product.

5 The government may guarantee loans and may also provide venture capital to entrepreneurs starting businesses. The government seeks to provide a business-friendly environment by, for example, reducing laws relating to small businesses. It also offers advice and support through organisations such as Business Link.

6 A franchise is the granting by one business to another individual or business of the rights to supply its products. A franchisor sells the business concept whilst the franchisee purchases the idea and the right to supply the products.

7 Copyright is the legal protection offered by the law to authors of written or recorded materials (e.g. books, films or music) for up to 70 years. A patent grants a business the sole right to benefit from an invention for a specified period. It provides the patent holder with the sole right to make and sell the product they have invented for a period of up to 20 years.

8 An entrepreneur is unlikely to have sufficient financial resources to start up a business. He or she will therefore require capital to purchase the assets that are required to start a business, such as property, vehicles, machinery and stock.

9 Adding value is the process of increasing the worth or value of some resources by working on them.

10 An entrepreneur might require a business plan:

- to apply successfully for a loan from a bank or other investor
- to help the entrepreneur judge whether the business is viable
- to monitor the performance of the business to check that it is meetings its targets

Chapter 2

Now test yourself

1 Primary market research:

Advantages
● It collects precisely the information that the business requires, which helps to ensure consumers receive the 'right' products.
● The data collected should be accurate as they have not been collected for other purposes or interpreted by other people.
● The data are not out-of-date as they will have been collected recently.

Disadvantages
● It is expensive as it can involve high labour costs in collecting and analysing data using techniques such as questionnaires.
● It can be time consuming to collect, especially if it is needed in a national market.

2 Qualitative market research is designed to discover the attitudes and opinions of consumers that influence their purchasing behaviour. A food manufacturer might use a consumer panel to test a new chocolate bar and receive detailed opinions on the taste and texture of the new product.

Quantitative market research is the collection of information on consumer views and behaviour that can be analysed statistically. This type of research might be used to investigate whether a new product is likely to achieve a sufficient volume of sales to make it financially viable.

3 A new business is unlikely to have sufficient finance to ask every potential customer their views on the proposed product. Hence, the entrepreneur will research a small proportion or sample of the market.

Random sampling means that each member of the population has an equal chance of being included. Quota sampling splits the population into a number of groups, each sharing common characteristics.

4 Different types of market:

Type of market	Explanation	Examples
Local markets	These are of a limited geographical area and used for products that are difficult to transport.	Painters and decorators and gardeners.
National markets	Firms in this type of market sell throughout the UK.	Builders such as Taylor Wimpey plc and retailers such as W H Smith Ltd.
Physical markets	This type of market is found in a precise location.	Portobello market in Notting Hill and your local market.
Electronic markets	The internet operates as a market for many small businesses, enabling them to reach a wide customer base.	eBay and Rightmove (a firm that promotes houses online).
Industrial markets	These are business-to-business markets where firms sell to one another.	Pilkington Glass sells to many businesses including house builders, and UK Coal plc sells its products to many businesses including those operating power stations.

5 Without sufficient levels of demand, a new business will not generate sufficient inflows of cash to pay bills as they become due, and in the longer term it will be unlikely to make a profit.

Actions to encourage higher levels of demand include:

- reduce prices (possibly)
- advertise more
- offer promotional deals such as 'buy one, get one free'.

6 Your mind map should show these seven market segments:

- age
- sex
- family size
- psychographic or lifestyle segmentation
- social class
- neighbourhood classification
- education

7 *Formulae:*

market share = the business's sales × 100/total market sales

market growth rate = change in market size × 100/original market size

Factors:

- Market share might rise if a firm reduces its prices or if competitors go out of business.
- Market share may fall if a firm's products become obsolete or if competitors increase their advertising.

8 Locational factors include the market, competition, infrastructure, technology, climate and natural resources, suppliers, costs and qualitative factors.

9 (i) A newly established take-away restaurant may have considered: the market, competition, suppliers and costs.

(ii) The farm may have taken into account: the market, infrastructure, climate and natural resources and costs.

Check your understanding

1 These items include: aims and objectives, resources required, market research plan, cash-flow forecast, budgets, sources of finance, etc.

2 Primary market research is likely to give higher-quality data as they are more up-to-date and have been collected for a specific purpose.

3 Qualitative market research.

4 Random sample.

5 To allow the entrepreneur to make a judgement as to the financial viability of the proposed business and to present in support of a loan application to a bank.

6 Market share is the percentage of total sales in a market which is achieved by one specific firm. Market size is the total demand for a particular product.

7 Market segmentation involves dividing a market into identifiable submarkets, each with its own customer characteristics. Sampling is the selection of a representative group of consumers from a larger population.

8 The costs involved, closeness to suitable sources of labour, infrastructure (electronic).

9 The results of market research, information from suppliers, personal information from CVs and information from secondary sources such as the internet and Mintel.

10 A low-cost location allows the business to make a profit as soon as possible and will help the business to manage its cash by minimising outflows.

Chapter 3

Now test yourself

1 Differences between corporate and non-corporate businesses:
- Corporate businesses have limited liability, unlike non-corporate businesses.
- Corporate businesses can sell shares and have shareholders.
- Corporate businesses (especially plcs) are generally much larger.

2 Advantages and disadvantages are:
- The entrepreneur and other owners will benefit from limited liability.

- The business can raise capital by selling shares.
- The business has to publish financial information, which may be of value to competitors.
- Private limited companies can only sell shares with the agreement of all existing shareholders.

3 Three objectives for a not-for-profit business:
- To help the local community possibly by providing essential services.
- To help people to acquire job-related skills to assist them into employment.
- To buy products from overseas under fair-trading schemes offering benefits to producers in less developed countries.

4 (i) Private limited companies may use: share capital, loans from banks and other investors, venture capital.

(ii) Sole traders and partnerships may use: personal sources of finance (possibly savings or redundancy pay), loans from friends and family and possibly loans from banks if they can be persuaded to invest.

5 (i) Share capital: when a company wishes to raise finance, when large sums are required and when ownership of the business and may not be an issue.

(ii) Loan capital: if a business has assets that can be used as collateral, if the bank or other investor has confidence in the business and if the business appears able to make repayments.

(iii) Venture capital: if the business is considered to be high risk, if the entrepreneur is in need of advice and if the business is a company and able to sell shares to the venture capitalist.

6 Advantages and disadvantages of employing people:

Financial reasons:
• Advantages: a business can have the skills of specialists which may increase revenue.
• Disadvantages include: increased costs of employment and training at a time when a business may have few financial resources.

Non-financial reasons:
• Advantages: possible increased sales as a result of employing specialists and also the ability for the entrepreneur to take holidays and breaks from the business.
• Disadvantages: the need to conform with UK and EU employment laws and the difficulty in selecting reliable employees.

Check your understanding

1 Corporate businesses have a legal identity that is separate from that of their owners.

2 Corporate businesses are private and public limited companies. Non-corporate businesses include sole traders and partnerships.

3 Temporary employees are only employed for a fixed period of time. Part-time employees work for less than full-time hours each week.

4 Sources include selling shares, loans from a bank, personal sources such as savings and loans from friends and family.

5 An overdraft is flexible as the business only pays interest on the amount that it borrows but it is repayable on demand.

Loans are normally for a fixed amount and repayable over a period of time.

6 There is a risk of losing control of the ownership and management of the business if other shareholders own in excess of 50% of the shares in the business.

7 Probably the major disadvantage is the absence of limited liability.

8 It is simple and cheap to establish a business as a sole trader as there are few legal restrictions.

9 Share capital can be used to raise large amounts of capital and interest does not have to be paid upon it. Dividends may be paid if sufficient profit has been earned.

10 Because many new businesses are considered to be risky and investors such as banks are unwilling to lend money. Further, as many new businesses are established as sole traders and partnerships they do not have the option of selling shares to raise capital.

Chapter 4

Now test yourself

1 Original total costs = £100,000 + (1,000 × £20) = £120,000
New total costs = £100,000 + (2,000 × £20) = £140,000
Difference = £20,000.

2 Sales revenue = 10,000 × £10 = £100,000
Total costs = £60,000 + (10,000 × £5) = £110,000
Loss = £10,000.

3 The contribution per unit = unit selling price − variable cost per unit
Product A = £10 − £6 = £4
Product B = £25 − £15 = £10

4 Formulae used in financial planning:
total costs = fixed costs + variable costs
revenue = quantity sold × selling price per unit
profit = sales revenue − total cost
contribution = sales revenue − variable costs
contribution per unit = unit selling price − variable cost per unit
breakeven output = fixed costs/contribution per unit

5 See Figure 4.3 (b) and (c) on p. 37.

6 Budgets may be necessary if the entrepreneur plans to arrange a loan with a bank as the bank will require evidence that the business can repay the loan.

Budgets will help an entrepreneur to assess whether the planned business is likely to make a profit.

It is more difficult for a new business to draw up budgets as it does not have financial records on which to base its forecasts.

The entrepreneur may lack experience in financial planning.

7 Market risks may occur because demand may be low because of reduced incomes and fears of unemployment.

Operating risks may centre on unreliable suppliers that may seek to reduce costs and supply substandard products or that may cease trading because of financial difficulties.

Financial risks may relate to shortages of cash as customers delay payments to protect their own cash reserves.

Check your understanding

1 Revenue is the total value of sales made by a business over a specified period of time.

2 A budget is a financial plan.

3 Fixed costs include rent and rates. Payments for raw materials and wages are examples of variable costs.

4 Contribution = sales revenue − variable costs.

5 Fixed costs = total costs − variable costs

6 Breakeven output = fixed costs/contribution per unit

7 As costs have risen a business will need to sell more units to reach breakeven output.

8 The revenue line will pivot upwards (allowing breakeven to be achieved at a lower level of output).

9 Its closing balance is (£2,500).

10 Total revenue = 150 × £250 = £37,500. Total costs = £1,200 + (150 × £90) = £14,700. Profit = £37,500 − £14,700 = £22,800.

11 Breakeven = £280,000/(£240 − £140) = 2,800 units of output.

12 Contribution per unit = (£2.50 − £1.90) = 60 pence. Total contribution = 60 pence × 100,000 = £60,000.

13 Because the level of sales (and hence output) will guide the entrepreneur in forecasting costs of production and hence profits or losses.

14 Breakeven analysis assumes that all output is sold and that all products are sold at a single price.

15 Because following an increase in price some consumers may decide not to purchase the product, leading to a decline in sales revenue.

16 Because it represents a payment to the entrepreneur as a reward for taking a risk in starting a business.

17 To assess the financial viability of the new business and in support of an application for a bank loan.

18 Market-based risks relate to the possibility of falling sales whilst operating risks refer to problems in production.

19 Possible objectives include bringing benefits to a community or engaging in fair-trading activities.

20 Many entrepreneurs do not plan their cash flows carefully and some new businesses offer customers too much time to pay to win their custom.

Chapter 5

Now test yourself

1 Causes of favourable and adverse variances:

Favourable variances	Response	Adverse variances	Response
Higher sales than expected	Increase production	Sales below forecast	Increase advertising
Lower fixed costs	Possibly reduce prices	Wage costs higher than forecast	Use more technology in production
Reduced fuel costs	Enjoy increased profits	Material costs higher than forecast	Seek new suppliers
Reduced material costs	Lower prices or enjoy higher profits	Profits below forecast	Seek new markets

2 Cash-flow problems:

Cause	Solution
Poor management	Training or recruiting skilled managers
Giving too much trade credit	Offer shorter periods or negotiate more favourable terms from suppliers
Overtrading	Plan the financial aspects of growth thoroughly
Unexpected expenditure	Have a contingency fund to meet such demands

3 Ways to increase profit margin:
- increase prices
- reduce costs
- improve capacity utilisation
- increase efficiency

4 Ways to increase profits:
- Introducing new products may result in a business increasing its sales, revenue and profit.
- Increasing capacity utilisation may increase revenue significantly with only a small increase in (variable) costs, thereby boosting profits.
- A reduction in fixed costs (possibly by moving to a cheaper location) may increase profits.

Check your understanding

1 A variance is the difference between planned activities in the form of budgets and the actual results that were achieved.

2 Favourable variances include profits above expectations and costs below forecasted levels.

3 Net profit margin.

4 A 10% figure is preferable as it represents a greater level of reward for the owners of a business.

5 Profits are the surplus of revenue over total costs for a trading period. Profitability is a measure which relates profits to some other factor such as sales revenue.

6 The airline could increase its price or improve capacity utilisation by having more passengers on each aeroplane.

7 It can use budgets to monitor its growth and check that it is meeting its targets. It will probably need loans to finance growth and budgets will provide evidence of the ability to repay loans.

8 The hotel may increase its advertising, improve the quality of its product or conduct market research to investigate the causes of the adverse variance.

Chapter 6

Now test yourself

1 (i) Operating wide spans of control:
- if managers are experienced
- if employees do not require close supervision
- if the employees are skilled and used to having some degree of delegation

(ii) Operating narrow spans of control:
- if the type of business means that close supervision is essential
- if the business traditionally has operated narrow spans of control
- if the employees are newly appointed and/or unskilled

2 (i) Internal recruitment:
- to increase the chance of selecting the best candidate
- if the business is seeking to minimise its costs (such as training)
- as a means of motivating employees

(ii) External recruitment:
- if the business is growing rapidly and recruiting many new employees
- if the business is seeking very high-quality employees or skills that are scarce
- if the business wishes to recruit people with new ideas

3 Your mind map may include topic areas such as those listed below.
- Cash-flow forecasts — recruitment and selection is likely to result in cash outflows.
- Customer service — recruiting employees with appropriate skills can improve the level of customer service.
- Productivity — recruiting people with the 'right' skills is likely to help to improve productivity levels.
- Skilled productive employees may allow a business to reduce its prices.

4 Advantages and disadvantages of training employees:

Advantages
● Improvement in skill levels and productivity
● Motivation may be enhanced
● Reduction in labour turnover

Disadvantages
● Cost can be substantial (especially for off-the-job training)
● Disruption to production
● Possibility of highly trained and skilled employees leaving to join rivals

5 External and internal motivation factors:
- External factors determine the level of motivation according to Taylor (finance) and also to Mayo to some degree (social factors).
- In contrast Herzberg and Maslow both believe that internal psychological factors are key influences on motivation within the workplace.
- Over time there has been a move towards those theories that support the view that internal stimuli determines motivation.
- You should decide whether internal or external stimuli are most important and think about why you have these beliefs.

6 Your mind map should include the following links:
- Taylor's theory — financial methods of motivation such as piece rate.
- Mayo's theory — teamworking.
- Herzberg — job enrichment and empowerment.

Check your understanding

1 The span of control is the number of subordinates for whom a manager is directly responsible.

2 The level of hierarchy refers to the number of layers of authority in an organisation.

3 Delegation is the passing of authority to a subordinate within the organisation. Authority is the power to carry out the task.

4 Supervisors provide a link between managers and shop-floor workers, and have responsibility for other employees. They may also have the authority to take certain decisions on routine issues. Team leaders carry out a similar role, but they may work alongside shop-floor workers.

5 Job descriptions set out the duties and tasks associated with a particular post. Person or job specifications set out the qualifications and qualities required of an employee.

6 Well-trained employees will be better motivated, as they feel valued and get a sense of achievement from performing their work more efficiently. Training improves employee performance, resulting in a more productive and efficient workforce.

7 Motivation can be seen as the will to work because of enjoyment of the work itself and therefore coming from within an employee. Alternatively it may be considered the desire to achieve a given target, because of some external stimulus.

8 Labour productivity = output per period/average number of employees

Labour turnover = number of employees leaving during a year × 100/average number of employees.

9 A chief executive is a vital appointment and is likely to have a huge influence on the future of the organisation. Appointing from the widest possible pool of applicants is a logical approach.

10 Teamworking offers a wide range of opportunities for social interactions, allowing employees to meet social needs at work.

11 Labour turnover = 50 × 100/250 = 20%.

12 The business may raise its wages, improve the quality and amount of its training or motivate employees using techniques such as empowerment.

13 An effective system might improve the productivity of the workforce by providing employees with the necessary skills. It may also motivate the workforce, improving performance if internal recruitment is used.

14 Empowerment may occur because managers wish to improve productivity levels to allow price reductions or to increase long-term profits. Alternatively it may be because a business wishes to improve levels of motivation to cut labour turnover.

15 The manager's decision may be because the business has cash-flow problems or because quality levels have reduced and it is important to avoid employees rushing production.

Chapter 7

Now test yourself

1 (i) Rationalisation:
- if the process is likely to generate substantial funds from the sale of assets
- if the level of sales is not expected to rise in the near future

(ii) Increasing sales:
- if it is possible to enter new markets without incurring excessive costs
- if the business is able to reduce prices to increase its sales
- if tastes and fashions are moving in favour of its products
- if the business is concerned about its corporate image (and job losses)

2 Advantages and disadvantages of implementing systems of quality control and quality assurance:

	Advantages	**Disadvantages**
Quality control	May be the cheaper option and can improve product design.	Only reveals faults at end of production process, increasing re-working costs.
Quality assurance	Can be motivational and likely to improve customer satisfaction.	Can be expensive to introduce because of training costs and may disrupt production.

Possible reasons for operating systems of quality assurance:
- can improve motivation by offering the opportunity to introduce other techniques such as teamworking
- may eventually reduce the organisation's labour costs by allowing wider spans of control

3 Your diagram might include:
- reference to the amount of trade credit offered and its effect on the company's cash-flow position
- mention of the supplier's price levels and impact on profit margins
- drawing links between a supplier's reliability and adaptability when a business is expanding

4 Some examples of the implications of a decision to use new technology:

(i) Marketing
New production processes allowing lower prices or new products increasing sales.

(ii) Finance
Initial costs possibly resulting in increased profits in the long term.

(iii) Operations management
The use of technology may assist a business in meeting its quality targets.

(iv) People in business
Production line technology may increase productivity.

Check your understanding

1 Unit costs = total costs/units of output

2 Quality is meeting the needs of a customer. Customer service is a range of activities designed to improve the degree of satisfaction experienced by a business's customers.

3 Quality control is the process of checking that completed production meets agreed criteria. Quality assurance ensures that quality standards are attained by all employees in a business.

4 A supplier provides a business with products and services that are essential for the organisation to carry out its commercial activities.

5 Capacity utilisation = current output per time period × 100/ maximum output per time period. The answer should be expressed as a percentage.

6 Computer-aided manufacture (CAM) operates when manufacturers use robots as an integral part of the production process. In contrast, computer-aided design (CAD) is used to plan and develop new product ideas.

7 A quality standard is awarded to businesses that have put into place certain systems that enable certain quality targets to be met.

8 By asking customers to complete online surveys, by telephoning customers who have recently bought a product to enquire about their experiences or by leaving monitoring cards for customers to complete.

9 One method is to increase sales to use up the available capacity. Entering new markets overseas might achieve this, or finding new uses for an existing product.

10 Non-standard orders occur when a customer asks for products that do not meet the normal specifications for that supplier. This may create operational problems if a business has to produce different products or different quantities. It may also lead to financial consequences if the business has to invest in new materials or equipment.

11 Implementing TQM might have a positive impact on motivation within a business. Employees might enjoy the job enlargement and enrichment that accompanies TQM. This may result in improved levels of productivity and reduced levels of absenteeism alongside the higher levels of quality.

12 It may be able to negotiate improved trade credit terms and possibly will be able to develop a wider range of suppliers in these circumstances.

13 Benefits may include the elimination of monotonous, repetitive tasks and fewer substandard products. Disadvantages may include the replacement of jobs by technology and smaller pay rises due to high expenditure on technology.

14 It may increase its capacity by using larger aircraft or by operating more flights.

15 There are likely to be high capital costs involved in the updating and it may need to make some employees redundant, possibly damaging its image.

Chapter 8

Now test yourself

1 Advantages and disadvantages of moving from a niche market into a mass market:

Advantages
● A business may benefit from higher levels of sales as a consequence.
● The business may also be able to reduce its unit costs (and increase profit margins) by producing large quantities of identical products.

Disadvantages
● The firm may face greater competition in a mass market, forcing it to, for example, reduce its prices.
● The business may have to spend heavily on promotion to establish itself in this larger market.

2 The Boston matrix allows businesses to undertake product portfolio analysis based on the product's market growth rate and its market share. It classifies products into four categories and helps managers to have products in each one.

The product life cycle is the theory that all products follow a similar pattern: moving through five stages during their life. Its use can avoid circumstances where firms have a range of products all in declining popularity.

3 Your diagram should show the following:

- Pricing strategies include: skimming, penetration, leadership and price taking.

- Influences include: price elasticity of demand, competitors' prices and the business's costs of production.

4 Techniques to improve a business's competitiveness:

(i) Marketing
Reducing prices, increasing promotion and developing new products.

(ii) Finance
Cutting production costs, improved cash-flow management, effective use of budgets.

(iii) Operations management
Increased capacity utilisation, improved levels of quality and enhanced levels of customer service.

(iv) People in business
Increased productivity, improved training and reduced levels of labour turnover.

Check your understanding

1 Marketing is the management process that identifies, anticipates and fulfils customer requirements efficiently and profitably.

2 Niche marketing occurs when businesses identify and satisfy the demands of small segments of a larger market. Mass marketing occurs when businesses aim their products at most of the available market.

3 The promotional mix includes advertising, public relations, direct selling and merchandising.

4 Four elements of the marketing mix are price, place, product and promotion.

5 Competitiveness is the extent to which a firm is successful in outperforming its rivals in the marketplace.

6 Barriers to entry may include price reductions, increased advertising and the launch of new products.

7 The price at which a business can sell relative to its rivals; whether or not the business's products possess USPs; the image that consumers have of the business in question.

8 Price-elastic demand exists when demand is sensitive to price changes. Price inelastic demand is the opposite, where demand is not responsive to price changes.

9 Pricing strategies are the medium- to long-term pricing plans that a business adopts, e.g. price penetration. Pricing tactics are a series of pricing techniques that are normally used only over the short term to achieve specific goals such as increasing sales, e.g. loss leaders.

10 Price skimming may be appropriate when a new product is launched onto the market, especially if it has unique points that differentiate it from rivals' products.

11 A cash cow is a product that has a large share of a market that is growing quickly. A problem child has a small share of a market that is growing quickly.

12 By engaging in environmentally friendly activities or offering high-quality training to all its employees.

13 Through developing unique features that differentiate them from competitors' products. Through advertising to stress the exclusive nature of its products.

14 The amount of finance available to this start-up business; the target market: for example, diners with low incomes.

15 Sales revenue might be high in the short term with little need for high expenditure on advertising. However, sales may decline sharply in the longer term if the products become less popular and the brewery will not have new products to replace them.